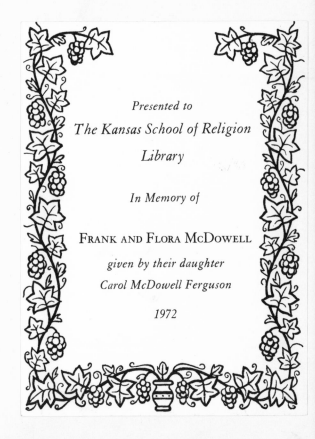

MODERN TRENDS IN ISLAM

MODERN TRENDS
IN ISLAM

By H. A. R. GIBB

OCTAGON BOOKS

A DIVISION OF FARRAR, STRAUS AND GIROUX

New York   1972

THE HASKELL LECTURES IN COMPARATIVE RELIGION
DELIVERED AT THE UNIVERSITY OF CHICAGO IN 1945
Copyright 1947 by The University of Chicago

Reprinted 1972
by special arrangement with The University of Chicago Press

OCTAGON BOOKS
A DIVISION OF FARRAR, STRAUS & GIROUX, INC.
19 Union Square West
New York, N. Y. 10003

Mohammedanism

LIBRARY OF CONGRESS CATALOG CARD NUMBER: 76-159188

ISBN 0-374-93046-5

Printed in U.S.A. by
NOBLE OFFSET PRINTERS, INC.
New York, N.Y. 10003

To the memory of

MOHAMMED HASANEIN ABDELRAZEK

in grateful remembrance
of twenty-five years of friendship

FOREWORD

FOR every student of Islam the Haskell Lectures are linked with the name of Duncan Black Macdonald. The present writer still recalls the eagerness and excitement with which he read for the first time those lectures delivered before the University of Chicago in 1906 and afterward published under the title of *The Religious Attitude and Life in Islam*. No other book has revealed so clearly, with such religious insight and such breadth of understanding, the springs of the spiritual life in the Muslim communion—its awareness of the unseen, its supernaturalism, its ascetic disciplines and mystical vocations, its superstitions and its manly puritanism.

It will be long before Professor Macdonald's analysis is outdated, but he himself was well aware of how much more was needed in this field. "It would be easy," he wrote in his concluding paragraph, "to outline further and certainly fruitful lines of investigation. The precise pathology of Muhammad's psychology is one. Another would be the history of the pantheistic development in the later Sufi schools, under Buddhistic and Vedantic influence—a wide field. A third would be as wide and still more weighty— the present religious attitudes and movements of the Muslim peoples. That in them are stirrings of new life, born of many causes, there can be no question."

Forty years have passed, but it cannot be said that striking progress has been made in any of these directions. To the study of Muhammad, as man and prophet, much new material has been brought, some of it of the first importance. But in the matter of Muhammad's psychology, subjective judgments and individual caprice still have the field all too much to themselves. On Sufism in general much new light has been thrown by the publication of texts and the studies of a number of scholars, among whom R. A. Nicholson and Louis Massignon are pre-eminent. But the specific point raised by D. B. Macdonald—pantheistic development in the later Sufi schools—still remains largely unexplored; and an immense area in the background of modern Muslim thought remains a blank for us, in consequence of this gap in our knowledge.

The third subject, the present religious attitudes and movements of the Muslim peoples, is the least-studied and most treacherous field of all. This may seem a paradox, when never before has the Muslim world been in such close contact with the Western nations and when never a year passes without the publication of several books, both in Europe and in America, dealing with one or other of the Muslim countries and peoples. To the Western student of the specifically religious aspects of modern Islamic culture, however, most of them offer little satisfaction.

The fullest documentation is to be found in the quarterly issues of the *Moslem World* since 1910. Though its standpoint and outlook are uncompromisingly missionary, it is a part of the modern missionary's technique to acquire a much deeper understanding of other religions than his predecessors displayed. Not all its contributors reach the high standard set by D. B. Macdonald, but a large proportion of its articles at least reflects current phases of Muslim religious thought. Other missionary journals add little to the materials contained in the *Moslem World*. In nonmissionary journals devoted to the East there is, as a rule, singularly little to be found on modern religious subjects; but an exception must be made for the *Revue du monde musulman*, published in Paris between 1906 and 1926, and its successor, the *Revue des études islamiques*, edited by Professor Louis Massignon.

In addition to these scattered raw materials, some valuable regional studies have been published by French scholars on North and West Africa and by Dutch scholars on the East Indies and one or two general pamphlets in French and German. In English there are two composite volumes of missionary studies, *The Vital Forces of Christianity and Islam* (1915) and *The Moslem World of Today* (1925), and another composite volume, *Whither Islam?* edited by the present writer in 1932. But of real books devoted to the significant movements in Islam, only two have appeared in the last quarter of a century. One of them, the work of Dr. Charles C. Adams of the American University at Cairo, published in 1933 under the title of *Islam and Modernism in Egypt,* offers a detailed survey of the movement associated with Shaikh Muhammad Abduh. The other, *Modern Islam in India,* is a candid and unsparing analysis of Muslim Indian movements in terms of social trends, written by a young Canadian scholar, Wilfred Cantwell Smith, and published at Lahore in 1943.

But since, after all, the subject of this investigation is what Muslims have been thinking and how their thoughts have been translated into acts, it might be expected that some Muslim writers would have been moved to explain at least to their fellow-Muslims, if not to the outer world, the nature of the intellectual revolution through which they were passing and how it has affected their thought on religious matters. Any expectations of this kind will be speedily disappointed. In the following pages the reader will find many references to articles, pamphlets, or books written by Muslims for Muslims. Had it not been for these, the task attempted here would have been impossible. But one looks in vain for any systematic analysis of new currents of thought in the Muslim world. Almost all the books written in English or French by Muslim writers, on the other hand, turn out to be apologetic works, composed with the object of defending Islam and demonstrating its conformity with what their writers believe to be present-day thought. The outstanding exception is the Indian scholar and poet, Sir Muhammad Iqbāl, who in his six lectures on *The Reconstruction of Religious Thought in Islam* faces outright the question of reformulating the basic ideas of Muslim theology.

From this brief survey of the printed materials available for the study of modern trends in Islam, it will be seen how few and, on the whole, how unsatisfying they are. It would indeed be impossible to construct any clear picture of the modern developments in Muslim thought out of their data alone. Something more is needed to serve as a basis or standpoint from which to view them and to relate them to one another, the more so because they belong to very different categories of evidence. As in all fields of historical research (and the subject is essentially a historical one), this additional source is the experience of the researcher and the personal qualities and equipment which he brings to the task.

At this present stage, therefore, one cannot hope to avoid the dangers and errors implicit in the attempt to generalize on the basis of a limited experience. No single person can possibly compass in his own direct knowledge all the varieties of faith and practice in the length and breadth of the Muslim world or think to enter into the minds of Berbers, Arabs, Turks, Persians, Afghans, Punjabis, and Bengalis, not to speak of Malays, Javanese, and the Negro peoples of East and West Africa. Even if the field is limited to the two most actively formative of the Muslim communities—the Arabs and the Indians—it must be confessed that all the information about Indian Islam in this book is at second hand. Yet this is perhaps a better position to be in than the reverse one; for, notwithstanding the greater numbers and the more varied intellectual activities among Indian Muslims, it is the Arabs who still constitute the real core of Islam.

One other word must be said, even at the risk of appearing too self-conscious. In these days, when we are enveloped in an atmosphere charged with propaganda, it is the

duty of every investigator to define precisely to himself and
to his audience the principles which determine his point of
view. Speaking in the first person, therefore, I make bold
to say that the metaphors in which Christian doctrine is
traditionally enshrined satisfy me intellectually as expressing symbolically the highest range of spiritual truth which
I can conceive, provided that they are interpreted not in
terms of anthropomorphic dogma but as general concepts,
related to our changing views of the nature of the universe.
I see the church and the congregation of Christian people
as each dependent on the other for continued vitality, the
church serving as the accumulated history and instrument
of the Christian conscience, the permanent element which
is constantly renewed by the stream of Christian experience and which gives both direction and effective power to
that experience.

My view of Islam will necessarily be the counterpart of
this. The Muslim church and its members constitute a
similar composite, each forming and reacting to the other
so long as Islam remains a living organism and its doctrines
satisfy the religious consciousness of its adherents. While
giving full weight to the historical structure of Muslim
thought and experience, I see it also as an evolving organism, recasting from time to time the content of its symbol-
ism, even though the recasting is concealed (as it is to a
considerable extent in Christianity) by the rigidity of its
outward formulas. The views expressed by living Muslims
are not to be discredited a priori by the argument that
these views cannot be reconciled with those of ninth-cen-
tury Muslim doctors. It is understandable that modern
Muslim theologians themselves should protest against innovations and should seek to tie Islam down to its medieval dogmatic formulations by denying, first of all, the possibility and, second, the legitimacy of the reconstruction of
Islamic thought. But it is certainly not for Protestant
Christians to refuse to Muslims, either as a community or

as individuals, the right to reinterpret the documents and symbols of their faith in accordance with their own convictions.

The practical conclusion from all this is that there is no possibility of avoiding the introduction of a very large subjective element into this discussion. But we can be on our guard against two frequent causes of misunderstanding. While none of us can help exteriorizing the feelings and beliefs of other people, especially those of a different communion or creed, when we discuss them, we ought at least to be aware that we are exteriorizing and that to that extent we are doing violence to the intimate personal element which constitutes the mainspring of the religious life.

In the same way the element of criticism inseparable from honest discussion makes it difficult to avoid the appearance of surveying the religious life of Muslims from some superior height. There is, indeed, no way to avoid it except by recognizing that we of the West are fellow-voyagers with them, engaged in a common spiritual enterprise, even though our ways diverge. The object of this inquiry is only to discover what progress they are making on their way. Though it may yield, at best, no more than a partial and provisional statement, it will serve its purpose if it directs attention to a question of the highest importance for the religious life of mankind.

In bringing this Foreword to an end, it is my pleasant duty to thank all those members and officers of the University of Chicago whose kindly assistance eased the difficulties of a wartime visit and who have materially helped the publication of these Lectures. In particular, I should wish to name Professor Eustace A. Haydon, Dean Carl F. Huth, and Dr. John A. Wilson of the Oriental Institute and the members of his staff. Among the latter I owe a special debt to Dr. G. von Grunebaum for reading and correcting the original proofs and guiding the preparation of the Index.

H.A.R.G.

Oxford
November 1946

TABLE OF CONTENTS

CHAPTER I

THE FOUNDATIONS OF ISLAMIC THOUGHT

IN SETTING out to survey the currents of religious thought among Muslims at the present day, we are faced at the start with a serious practical difficulty. No movement of thought takes place in a void. Whether the impulses which affect it from without are many and powerful or few and weak, they are related in the mind of the subject to a habit of thought and a system of ideas which are already there. We cannot hope to follow with any understanding the modern movements in Islam unless we set them against an established background of Islamic ideas.

It would seem self-evident that the only satisfactory background must be the state of Islam in the nineteenth century, or, at the earliest, Islam in the eighteenth century. But these are subjects on which our knowledge is still limited by immense gaps. The usual practice of writers on Islam is to concentrate on the early centuries of theological and legal development and sectarian conflicts and the rise of the Sufi movement and brotherhoods. After the thirteenth century or so, it is assumed that, from a religious angle, Islam stayed put—that it remained fixed in the molds created for it by the scholars, jurists, doctors, and mystics of the formative centuries and, if anything, decayed rather than progressed.

In some respects this view is apparently justified, and it is, indeed, held by a number of modern Muslim scholars themselves. But no great organization of human belief, thought, and will really stands still over a period of six centuries. It is true that the external formulations of the Muslim faith have shown little development during the whole of these six centuries. Yet, in fact, the inner structure of Muslim religious life was being profoundly readjusted and, as in other religious communities, the process generated an expansive energy which found outlets in several different kinds of activity.

Consider only the external evidences of vitality which Islam showed during this time—the establishment of the Ottoman Empire in the Near East and of the Mogul Empire in India, the revival of Shi'ism in Persia, the expansion into Indonesia and the Malay Peninsula, the growth of the Muslim community in China, the expulsion of the Spanish and Portuguese from Morocco, the extension of the Islamic belt in East and West Africa. The older historians were liable to regard all or most of these as military movements pure and simple; and the element of military power and conquest which they contain must not, of course, be left out of view. Even so, a conquering and expanding faith is a living faith, not a mere dry husk of belief and practice. We now know, too, better than before, the role played by this living faith, first in anticipating and then in helping to build up the military power, in molding the inner structure and organization of empire, and in repairing the ravages of war and reknitting the social fabric.

In the next chapter an attempt will be made to trace in outline the character of the internal evolution in Islam between the thirteenth and the nineteenth centuries. This by itself will not wholly overcome the difficulty with which we are confronted. Yet it may serve the purpose if, leaving detail aside, the general process can be seen in relation to the fundamental terms and categories of Islamic thought. This method of approach to the problem, however, requires, in the first place, some analysis and definition of the concepts and attitudes which underlie the formulation and the religious institutions of Islam. It is all the more important to make this effort, since these characteristic features have a direct bearing not only on the medieval but also on the modern developments within Islam. Modernism itself is the outcome of certain changes in the character of religious thought; and much of the argument for and against modernism is related, consciously or unconsciously, to those first principles which lie at the roots of the Muslim structure of belief and practice.

The basis of all Muslim thought about religion is, of course, the Koran. The Koran is not, like the Bible, a collection of books of widely different dates and by many different hands. It is a volume of discourses delivered by Muhammad during the last twenty years or so of his life, consisting mainly of short passages of religious or ethical teaching, arguments against opponents, commentaries on current events, and some rulings on social and legal matters. Muhammad himself believed that all these utterances were inspired, since they were not shaped by his own conscious thought. By him, as by all Muslims of his own time and of later ages, they were taken to be the direct word of God, dictated to him through the angel Gabriel. After what Professor Duncan Black Macdonald has said about the closeness of the unseen world to the Semitic mind and about the Eastern conception of prophecy, it would be superfluous for me to trace further the psychological presuppositions of this belief.

Yet we should be seriously mistaken if we were to regard it as merely a theological dogma which has been inherited, generation after generation, for thirteen hundred years. On the contrary, it is a living conviction which ever renews and confirms itself in the heart and mind of the Muslim, and more especially the Arab, as he studies the sacred text.

Muslim orthodoxy has generally been opposed to the translation of the Koran even into other Islamic languages, although the Arabic text is sometimes accompanied by interlinear translations in Turkish, Persian, Urdu, and so forth.[1]* This attitude is supported by theological reasoning, which is quite self-consistent but possibly rationalizes to some extent objections derived from rather different considerations, for the Koran is essentially untranslatable, in the same way that great poetry is untranslatable. The seer can never communicate his vision in ordinary language. He can express himself only in broken images, every inflection of which, every nuance and subtlety, has to be long and earnestly studied before their significance breaks upon the reader—images, too, in which the music of the sounds plays an indefinable part in attuning the mind of the hearer to receive the message. To paraphrase them in other words can only be to mutilate them, to substitute clay for fine gold, the plodding of the pedestrian intelligence for the winged flight of intuitive perception—at least until long familiarity, as in the case of the Latin and English translations of the Hebrew and Greek Scriptures, has given the new words something of the same emotive power, independently of the structure (and sometimes even of the meaning) of the originals.

An English translation of the Koran must employ precise and often arbitrary terms for the many-faceted and jewel-like phrases of the Arabic; and the more literal it is, the grayer and more colorless it must be. In passages of plain narrative, legislation, and the like, the loss may be less great, although not only the unevennesses and the incohesions of the compilation but also the fine shades, the hammer strokes, and the eloquent pauses (if they can be reproduced at all) may have a disconcerting or, as Carlyle said, a "crude and incondite" effect. Even in so simple a sentence as "Verily We give life and death and unto Us is the journeying," it is impossible to present in English (or perhaps any other language) the force of the five-times-repeated "We" in the six words of the original.[2] Allowing for all this, however, we shall still not grasp what the Koran

* The footnotes are at the end of the book.

means to the Arab until we make an effort to appreciate the part that language plays in determining his psychological attitudes.

The spring of mental life among the Arabs, as among other peoples, is furnished by the imagination, expressing itself in artistic creation. One often hears it said that the Arabs have no art. If art is confined to such things as painting and sculpture, the charge may be true. But this would be a despotic and unjustifiable limitation of the term. Art is any production in which aesthetic feeling expresses itself, and it is doubtful whether any people is totally devoid of artistic expression in some form or another, whether it be in music or dancing or ceramics or the visual arts. The medium in which the aesthetic feeling of the Arabs is mainly (though not exclusively) expressed is that of words and language—the most seductive, it may be, and certainly the most unstable and even dangerous of all the arts. We know something of the effect of the spoken and written word upon ourselves. But upon the Arab mind the impact of artistic speech is immediate; the words, passing through no filter of logic or reflection which might weaken or deaden their effect, go straight to the head. It is easy, therefore, to understand why Arabs, to whom the noble use of speech is the supreme art—and other Muslims also, to whom by long familiarity the Arab sensitivity to its language has become second nature—should see in the Koran a work of superhuman origin and a veritable miracle.

Further, the Arab artistic creation is a series of separate moments, each complete in itself and independent, connected by no principle of harmony or congruity beyond the unity of the imagining mind. Western art, especially since the Middle Ages, has developed a whole series of complicating techniques—drama superimposed on romance, mass in place of line, polyphony in place of homophony in music —which make of the artistic creation a harmony or synthesis of multiple elements, appealing to the refined intelligence as well as to the emotions. The art of speech, on the other hand, among ourselves as well as among the Arabs, still retains its simple and discrete (we might even call it "primitive") character; and because of this it exerts a far more intense power of appeal to the imagination both of the individual and of the mass, a power which may even be so great as to inhibit the capacity to form a synthesis.

Among all developing peoples, however, the creative impulses of the imaginative life must be furnished with an intelligible object or direction. This function is assumed by one of two forces, namely, religious intuition and rational thought. I should not like to assert that these alternatives are by necessity mutually exclusive; but it is a matter of experience that, apart from cases of special genius, individuals or societies incline generally to the one or to the other. Nor do I mean to exclude religion from the rational life; but, whereas the intuitive life is directed either by religion or by sheer subjective fantasy (which is to say, by nothing at all), the rational life comprehends religion as only one of its objects.

There could be no question as to which of these two would more immediately attract and move the Arab mind, in view of its inherited awareness of the unseen world and the powerful stimulus of the Koran. Besides all this, the outward simplicity and concreteness of the ideas of the Koran corresponded to the simplicity and concreteness of their imaginative life, and its code of ethics set up a practical ideal, which harmonized with and satisfied their social aspirations. Consequently, all their intellectual powers were directed into the effort to build up the structure of the religious institution of Islam and to make it dominant in every relationship of social life as it already dominated their mental life.

But this endeavor called for the exercise of a different set of faculties. The artistic imagination cannot construct a system. That is the task of reason. Now it is very frequently observed both in individuals and in nations that the very qualities in which they excel entail, and may even be the result of, the defect of other qualities. The student of Arabic civilization is constantly brought up against the striking contrast between the imaginative power displayed, for example, in certain branches of Arabic literature and the literalism, the pedantry, displayed in reasoning and exposition, even when it is devoted to these same productions. It is true that there have been great philosophers among the Muslim peoples and that some of them were Arabs, but they were rare exceptions. The Arab mind, whether in relation to the outer world or in relation to the processes of thought, cannot throw off its intense feeling for the separateness and individuality of the concrete events. This is, I believe, one of the main factors lying behind that "lack of a sense of law" which Professor Macdonald regarded as the characteristic difference in the oriental.

It is this, too, which explains—what it is so difficult for the Western student to grasp—the aversion of the Muslims from the thought-processes of rationalism. The struggle between rationalism and intuitive thought for control of the Muslim mind was fought out, for the first time, over the postulates of Greek speculative philosophy in the early centuries of Islam. The intellectual consequences of that conflict were decisive. They not only conditioned the formulation of the traditional Muslim theology but set a permanent stamp upon Islamic culture; and they still lie behind the conflicts arising in more recent years out of direct contact with modern Western thought. The rejection of rationalist modes of thought and of the utilitarian ethic which is inseparable from them has its roots, therefore, not in the so-called "obscurantism" of the Muslim theologians but in the atomism and discreteness of the Arab imagination.

Consequently, the Arabs—and with them the Muslims

generally—were compelled to distrust all abstract or a priori universal concepts, such as the "Law of Nature" or ideal "Justice." Such concepts they branded (and not unjustly) as "dualism" or "materialism," based on false modes of thought which could produce but little good and much evil. We shall see later how the great Muslim revivalist of the nineteenth century, Jamāl ad-Dīn al-Afghāni, emptied the vials of his wrath upon those Indian modernists who tried to prove the truth of Islam by arguing its "conformity with nature." Although the Muslim scholastics found such auxiliary disciplines as logic and mathematics useful, and to that extent adopted and encouraged the "scientific" mode of thought, they kept them closely confined to a subordinate status; and the stricter theologians—like Ibn Taimīya, who wrote a "Refutation of Logic"—were unwilling to concede even so much.

On the other hand—if I may diverge for a moment—the concentration of Arab thought upon the individual events fitted Muslim scholars to develop the experimental method in science to a degree far beyond their predecessors in Greece and Alexandria. This is a subject on which I am not competent to enlarge; but it is, I think, generally agreed that the detailed observations of Muslim investigators materially aided the progress of scientific knowledge and that it was from them that the experimental method was introduced or restored to medieval Europe. In the other aspect of science, however, the combination of the results of observation and experiment and the dovetailing of them into self-consistent ideal structures, held together by the concept of natural laws, the Muslim scientists were, of course, hampered by the very qualities in which they excelled, besides being to some extent inhibited by theological dogmas.

To revert now to Muslim religious thought, we should expect to find these same qualities of imagination and literalism displayed in the development of the theological system and its social applications. We do, in fact, see it very clearly in the interpretation of the Koran; but a simpler example will be found in the treatment of the person, acts, and sayings of Muhammad. Under the impulse of veneration for the Prophet and for his office, the religious imagination begins to elaborate its conception of what a prophet should be—sinless, for example, and endowed with miraculous powers; and as it progressively raises its standards, literalism obediently toils up behind it, producing out of the stores of tradition and by interpretation of koranic verses the evidences and proofs required to consolidate the concept as a theological dogma. The religious imagination, not content with accepting the inspiration of the Koran, insists that the inspiration of the Prophet cannot end there; this would be to allow too much scope to his mere humanity and possibly, therefore, his liability to err. In all that he said and did he must be, at least tacitly, inspired, and every action must be capable of serving as the model for human action in the same sphere. The scholars, intent on expanding the doctrinal and legal systems based on the Koran and needing for these purposes the additional materials supplied by the tradition, formally incorporate it in the theological structure as a second infallible source. Then they build up a vast and intricate science by which spurious traditions can be detected and rejected and the accepted traditions can be classified in categories of "good," "less good," and "weak."

Already in this connection we meet the difficulty that we shall encounter elsewhere about the relation between inner reality and outer form. It is easy to drive a coach and horses through the whole fabric of this elaborate "science of tradition." Many Muslim scholars themselves in the early centuries were uneasy about it. Yet ultimately it was accepted, because (broadly speaking) the external rules were, to a large extent, only a formal method of stabilizing and rationalizing what the conscience of the Muslim community already accepted. Thus and thus is what the Prophet could have been expected to say in given circumstances or in answer to given questions; if traditions existed in the contrary sense, they must be spurious, or at least (if the rules made it impossible to reject them as spurious) they must be "harmonized" or else discarded as having been "abrogated." I have no doubt in my own mind that the older tradition does, in fact, reflect the mind of Muhammad to a greater or less extent, though many who are better qualified to judge than I am hold a different view. But it is precisely because the tradition as a whole has been used to validate, instead, the outlook and opinions of the early generations of Muslims that so many schools of modernists reject its authority altogether and adopt the slogan "Back to the Koran."

The way in which the corpus of tradition was shaped to serve the ends of the Muslim religious consciousness vividly illustrates a third characteristic of Muslim thought. I find it difficult to define its nature precisely, because of the misleading associations of all the relevant words in English. Thus we are frequently told, on the one hand, that Islam is authoritarian, and so in a sense it is, as we shall see in the fifth chapter. On the other hand, Muslim apologists proclaim with conviction that Islam is democratic, which is true also, provided the political sense of the term is not insisted on. That the ordinary business of secular government is to be controlled by the general body of believers is an idea which was, indeed, formulated in the first century of Islam, but only to be decisively rejected as heretical, because of the excesses of its supporters. Not even the theoretical equality of all Muslims, though supported by several texts of the Koran, is enough to prove its political democracy.[3] But in religious matters the humblest Muslim stands on a level with the caliph or his chief *qadi*, and the ultimate control rests with the conscience of the people as a whole. *Vox populi*, the expressed will of the community—not as measured by the counting of votes or the decisions of councils at any given moment, but as demonstrated by the slowly accumulating pressure of opinion over a long period of time—is recognized in orthodox Islam next after *Vox Dei* and *Vox Prophetae* as a third infallible source of religious truth.

This principle is known as *ijmā^c*, the "consensus of the community." There were those who tried to limit it to the consensus of the learned. But a striking incident in the seventeenth century showed how futile the consensus of the learned was, even when supported by the secular power, against the pressure of public opinion. When the use of coffee began to spread in the Near East the jurists almost unanimously took the view that coffee-drinking was unlawful and punishable with the same penalties as wine-drinking, and a number of persons were actually executed for indulging in this vicious practice.[4] But the will of the community prevailed, and today coffee is freely consumed even by those puritans who reject *ijmā^c* in principle altogether.

It should be clear why *ijmā^c* has always been a subject of controversy between the conservative and the modernizing wings in Islam. Consensus is by no means a liberal principle; on the contrary, it is a principle of authority. What the community says may not be gainsaid. But because its authority is formally invoked only for what is not formally or explicitly authorized by the Koran or by the tradition, and because it is therefore an authority which may and does sanction what are called "innovations," the stricter theologians of all ages from the third century of Islam to the Wahhabis of today reject the claims made for it and confine its validity to the first generation of Muslims only, while the modernists of all ages have relied upon it to provide their eventual justification.[5]

These are, then, the three "roots of the Faith" in Islam

—Koran, tradition, and consensus; and by their interaction not only the whole structure of doctrine has been built up but also the structure of the socioreligious institution and of religious thought itself. I said just now that consensus was a principle of authority, since it can be (and often has been) used to circumscribe the range of permissible belief and practice. But within limits it is also a principle of toleration. Just because it rests upon the conscience of the whole body, it follows that no one group of Muslims holding a particular view, however powerful it may be, is entitled to declare the views held by any other group to be heretical or, if it should do so, to attempt to suppress the other views by force. The only sectaries in Islam (excluding the syncretist sects, such as Babism, Bahaism, and the original Ahmadīya movement in India, which have definitely broken away from the basic tenets of Islam) are those who, rejecting *ijmāᶜ*, have sought to impose their own doctrines by violence. Had the Shiᶜites been content with peaceful propaganda instead of fomenting revolution and insulting the beliefs of the Sunni majority, I think it almost certain that their doctrine would have been recognized as equally orthodox, and the split between Sunni and Shiᶜi would have been narrowed in course of time, just as the divergences within the Sunni community itself have been gradually reduced by the operation of "consensus."

The counterpart of *ijmāᶜ*, or consensus, is *ijtihād*, "exercise of judgment," which has been called by Iqbāl the "principle of movement" in Islam. But it is important for us to understand exactly what *ijtihād* means and the role which it has played in the history of Muslim religious thought. To begin with, it in no way implies, as some modernists would like us to believe, "freedom of judgment." The word literally means "exerting one's self," in the sense of striving to discover the true application of the teachings of Koran and tradition to a particular situation, and it may not go against the plain sense of these teachings. The orthodox theologians, fearing that to recognize the legitimacy of *ijtihād* might open the door to individual reinterpretation and schism, have always done their best to limit its scope. According to the classical doctrine, the range of *ijtihād* was progressively narrowed down, as successive generations of doctors, supported by "consensus," filled up the gaps in the doctrinal and legal systems. Finally, no more gaps remained to be filled, or only very insignificant ones, and thereupon "the gate of *ijtihād* was closed," never again to be reopened.[6]

By this means the scholastics applied an effective brake to the "principle of movement." Nevertheless, many reformers dared the ban and claimed the right of *ijtihād*. Here again we are faced with a paradox. Their claim is, of course, worthless unless it is supported by *ijmāᶜ*. But it is precisely against *ijmāᶜ* that they have raised their voices, against (that is to say) the doctrine that matters of belief and practice have been irrevocably determined by the consensus of the community in past generations. They assert that later generations cannot be bound by what they regard as the errors of past generations. Those modernists who claim the "right of *ijtihād*," the right to reject the theological constructions of the Middle Ages and to reinterpret the sources in the light of modern thought, may have at least an arguable case. But their action remains purely individual, personal, and therefore negligible unless they can secure the approval of *ijmāᶜ*. And it is a significant fact that the only claimants to *ijtihād* whose claims have been supported by some measure of consensus have been those who rejected certain of the beliefs or practices sanctioned by *ijmāᶜ*, not in order to modernize the doctrines of Islam, but in order to return to the practice of the primitive community.

However that may be, it is at least a striking feature of Sunni Islam that it tolerates, and indeed almost boasts of, the existence of differences of opinion within the community. The most familiar example is that of the four schools of law, called Hanafi, Māliki, Shāfiʿi, and Hanbali after the four jurists of the second and third centuries who are regarded as their founders, and all considered equally orthodox. All four systems, for example, are taught in the university mosque of al-Azhar at Cairo. It is true that the differences among them come down mostly to relatively minor points of law and ritual, although the Hanbalis, with their more intense opposition to all "innovations," theoretically reject ijmāʿ in all but its narrowest sense and have at times shown some intolerance of other opinions. But this recognition of the four schools is by no means the only, or the most remarkable, example of the readiness of the Sunni community to admit a measure of freedom of conscience. We shall have occasion to deal in the next chapter with the much deeper division between the scholastic and the mystical theologies which have existed side by side in orthodox Islam for many centuries.

More particularly, this catholic tendency has a direct bearing on the main question with which we are concerned, the rise of modernist movements; for, however much the conservative theologians may attack or even strive to suppress the heresies of the modernists, the issue does not rest with them but with the community as a whole.[7] And the community as a whole shows little inclination to be thrown off its balance. Although there have been cases of the formal condemnation of individual opinions as heretical, the modernists have, generally speaking, had to suffer little more than abuse from their conservative opponents, whose intemperate language is often itself a confession of their disappointment at the lack of support which they find in public opinion.

The conviction underlying ijmāʿ, that religion is best left in the safekeeping of the consciences of ordinary intelligent believers, and its corollary of toleration of differ-

ences on secondary points seem also to explain one striking difference between the religious institutions of Christianity and Islam. I mean the absence of a hierarchy and
of all that organization of councils, synods, and sees which
plays so large a part in the history of the Christian church.
It may be that this lack of organization is to be related to
that atomism of the Arab mind which we have already discussed, but it is a point on which I do not feel competent
to express an opinion. I should prefer to base it rather on
historical grounds, remembering that Islam became the expression of a deep social reaction among the peoples of the
Near East not only against the intolerance of the Byzan-
tine and Zoroastrian priesthoods but also against the im-
position of social and legal institutions which conflicted
with their own social instincts and ideals.

Finally, we must take into account the influence both of
social tradition and of social change. If we recall that the
Islamic peoples are the heirs of some of the oldest societies
in the world, societies which have had a continuous existence for over five thousand years and which, in spite of
migrations and revolutions, have preserved an astonishing
measure of stability, we must surely concede their possession of a highly developed social instinct and respect it. I
would suggest that the secret of their success lies in their
recognition that any social structure, if it is to be both
solidly based and elastic enough to meet disasters and
crises, must rest on a general will, not on enforced consent
or on complex organizations, and that a general will can be
built up only by gradual stages over a period of many generations. Since, of all the instruments for forging a general
will, religion is the most powerful, there will always be a
tendency in such societies to entwine their social institutions with their religion, and to cement the whole structure
by respect for the religious "tradition." In a society so
established, tradition then becomes so powerful a force
that individual aberrations or partial movements of op-

position are ineffectual in face of the mass, and negligible unless they resort to violent measures.

The presupposition, then, of the toleration of differences and looseness of organization associated with the concept of "consensus" is a society characterized by what we should call a "conservative" outlook, not an unchanging society but one in which changes are resisted and come about only by slow and imperceptible stages. It would clearly be impossible to attain or to attach authority to a "general will" if the outlook of society were constantly changing or characterized by a readiness to change. The East has known such times, too—times when new ideas have broken through the crust of old traditions, as Islam itself most strikingly proved by supplanting the older religions and social traditions of Asia.

When these new stresses arise and the old social structure begins to show cracks, men's minds are naturally confused by conflicting counsels. Shall they pull down the old building and hurriedly erect a new one? Or clamp the old walls together and fill in the cracks? Or patch it up with new bricks here and there? Above all, are the old foundations still sound? If the old building must come down, can they serve for the new one? The present is just such a time of change, conflict, and confusion in Muslim society. None of us can tell what will come out of it. In the following chapters the most I can hope to do is to give a general picture of what is going on and to draw attention to what appear to me to be the more significant details.

CHAPTER II

THE RELIGIOUS TENSION IN ISLAM

IN ALL living religion there is a tension. The cause lies in the religious consciousness itself, with its line of division between the worshiped and the worshiper, its sense of the holy and its sense of sin. All religion asserts the otherness of God. But, at the same time, the worshiper is conscious of the nearness of God, of the impossibility of separating the idea of God from his own spiritual experience. In the foundation deeds of individual religions, the teaching of their founders, these two elements exist side by side, synthesized in greater or less degree, since it is from the intimate union of the two elements in their own spiritual experience that their creative power is derived. But in the lives of their followers the tension springs up afresh. We know how vividly, for example, it is expressed in the letters of Paul. In the history of every developed religious community some few great and deep thinkers may again attain to a synthesis—partial and provisional though it may be—of these two fundamental and seemingly opposed conceptions. The great majority, however, will lean either to one side or to the other and will worship either a more transcendental God or a more immanent God; and, though the choice is frequently determined by individual feeling and response, this inclination may even be institutionally organized, as, for example, in Calvinism and Quakerism.

In Islam, too, this tension is present. In the Koran the transcendence of God is asserted again and again with an absoluteness which seems to leave no possible loophole for a doctrine of immanence. Yet this unimaginable transcendence does not exclude the attributes of love and "subtlety," whereby the Divine is so interfused with the spiritual life of men that God "is closer to man than his own neck-vein." I need not retrace here in detail, when it has already been so brilliantly done by Professor Macdonald and others, the history of the struggle in the Islamic church between these two conceptions of God. For our present purpose it is necessary only to note more particularly one or two special features which have given to the conflict of the two principles within Islam its peculiar character and which still affect the religious attitude and outlook of Muslims.

There is a recurrent tendency in Islamic thought to erect speculative systems by forcing a logical argument to what we should regard as excessive lengths. Starting from a given concrete premise, the argument is carried forward by successive syllogisms until, as Professor Macdonald has said, "a theory of all things in heaven and earth would be developed from this single idea." This danger, I need hardly remark, is one that especially besets systems of theology. The earliest theologians in Islam were scholars who had been suddenly introduced to Greek philosophy and, under its fascination, set out to systematize the teachings of the Koran in agreement with the doctrines of Aristotle and the Neo-Platonists. It was a perfectly legitimate object. That is what theology is for—to state the truths of religion (which are, so far, only intuitively known) in terms of the highest intellectual concepts of the time. But one thing the theologian may not do. He may not, on the pretext of accommodating religion and philosophy, question the truths he has set out to defend. At this point theology stops short. But these early Muslims went on, with the result that the great body of believers was outraged. The orthodox theologians evolved, in their turn, a dialectic weapon; to the cutting edge of Greek logic they fitted, in place of the universals of Greek speculative thought, the positive doctrines of the Koran, and with this they ultimately drove the Hellenizers from the field.

We have already seen that this was the decisive moment in the history of Muslim civilization—the moment at which Islam rejected the conceptions which were, later on, to exercise a determining influence in Western civilization. The moral effect of that victory still gives comfort and assurance to the orthodox ulema of the present day in their struggle against the influence of the Western philosophies, which they are somewhat rashly tempted to identify with the old Greek philosophies. But the orthodox theologians misunderstood the reasons for their success. It was not any intrinsic superiority in their logic but the intuitive clinging of the mass of the community to the truths of the Koran that really defeated the Hellenizers. That the Koran is anticlassical in spirit seems to me undeniable; to that extent the popular and the scholastic reactions were in harmony.

But when the scholastics, in their triumph, went on to construct a perfectly unassailable fortress of argument and proof, they, too, were compelled to cement their system with a large element of Greek rationalism. In their struggle with the Hellenizers, they had been defending the doctrine of the transcendence of God. Their opponents, it is true, had asserted themselves to be the true transcendentalists and had charged the orthodox with assenting to a crudely anthropomorphic interpretation of koranic metaphor. But in the judgment of the orthodox the simple anthropomorphism which speaks of God in terms of the human figure was far less dangerous than the anthroposophism which reasons about God in terms of human wisdom. Overemphasizing, then, as is the way of controversialists, the otherness of God, they constructed their new logical fortress with such stubbornly transcendentalist materials that it turned into a vast cold monument, beneath which the element of personal religious experience seemed to be crushed out of existence. Fortunately for Islam, it was not to be so. The monumental edifice survived as the official Muslim theology; but to the great body of the orthodox neither philosophy nor logic had any meaning, and theology was a wolf in sheep's clothing. The true believer believed "without asking why."

There is in all this a strangely close analogy with the struggle between the Averroists and the Christian ecclesiastical authorities in the thirteenth and fourteenth centuries, followed by the monumental *Summa* of Thomas Aquinas and the complete failure of both Averroists and Thomists to produce any effect on the general body of Christians, who remained (as Professor Gilson might say) unregenerate Tertullianists. The analogy goes even further; for, just as the revulsion against the disputes of the Christian theologians produced, on the one hand, the "New Devotional" movement and, on the other, the mystical doctrines associated with Meister Eckhart, so in Islam, alongside the cultivation of simple piety, there grew up also the mystical movement known as "Sufism." But from this point the course of development in the two religions diverged widely.

The function of Sufism was to restore to the religious life of the Muslim the element of personal communion with God which orthodox theology was squeezing out. It was not long, however, before precisely the same current of exaggeration set in here, too. For a moment it was dammed up by the religious genius of al-Ghazāli (d. A.D. 1111), who created a new synthesis between the two poles of the religious consciousness by rebuilding the structure of orthodox theology upon the foundations of personal religious experience. But only for a moment; then the theologians returned, high and dry, to their transcendental mausoleum, while the mystics plunged on down the rapids that ended in the whirlpool of pantheism.

From that time on, there were two recognized systems of

theology in Islam—the transcendentalist and the monist, one that developed to extremes the doctrine of the otherness of God and one that asserted His immanence in every part of nature. Whether the extremism which produced this strange result was due (as Dr. Macdonald has asserted[1]) to the absolute unitarianism of the koranic doctrine of God or (as I prefer to believe) to the categories and character of Eastern thought is, for the present, immaterial to us. But two observations must be made. The first is the point with which I began, that Muslim systematizers do, in fact, display this tendency to logical extremism, irrespective of whether the conclusions of the systems so evolved can be unified or organically related to one another. The second point is (if I may make bold to say so) that the resulting theologies are very often divorced from the beliefs and practices of the great body of Muslims. To judge from the books, one would suppose that the Muslim must be either a complete transcendentalist or a complete pantheist. It may be confidently said that the average sincere Muslim keeps, much more than do his professional guides, to the middle of the road.

It has always seemed to me erroneous to assume that the theological formulation of any Islamic doctrine exactly expresses a living reality in the thought and practice of the Muslim community, though I should not deny it a priori at every point. It is, indeed, one of the most confusing features in the Islamic system that the relation between outward formulation and inner function or reality is often a curiously indirect one. We in the West are constantly apt to be led astray by taking these formulations at their face value and applying our own logic to them, forgetting that in every formulation of thought and doctrine there is a necessary element of metaphor, inseparable from the nature of human speech. Very probably, too, many modernists in the East are as often led astray by not recognizing the metaphors in our speech, just as it is largely because of this unrecognized element of metaphor that the logical argument, when pushed to extremes, is carried off its feet and swung into the realm of pure concept.[2]

The orthodox doctrine of predestination, for example, is, in its theological formulation, derived from a series of logical propositions intended to exclude the faintest suggestion of any theoretical limitation upon the power of God and supported by the dominant (but by no means exclusive) tendency in the koranic passages relating to the problem of free will. This doctrine is commonly asserted to be the cause of what is called "Muslim fatalism." I suspect that something may possibly be said on behalf of the converse view; and, in any case, Muslim "fatalism" does not go very much beyond that found in any community (Muslim, Christian, or Hindu) in which poverty and ignorance breed resignation in the face of bodily ills, physical disasters, and the violence of tyrants. The ordinary Muslim takes thought for the morrow, like any other man; he assumes, like other civilized persons, that given actions will produce given results;[3] and even in the matter of his future in the next life he takes predestination much more lightly than the Calvinist, since he believes that, whoever they may be whom God has predestined to hell fire, they are certainly not to be found in the orthodox Muslim community.

Likewise, the ordinary Muslim is no pantheist in any precise sense of the term, notwithstanding the sensuous imagery of the great Persian poets and the influence they have exercised in India and Turkey, as well as in Persia. But there is in the mental makeup of nearly all the Muslim peoples a strong infusion of what we may call the "raw material of pantheism." I mean the heritage of primitive animism, the belief in spirits, in *jinns*, in *afrīts*, in all those mysterious and magical powers which Dr. Macdonald analyzed in his Haskell Lectures. And though some of these animistic beliefs and practices were definitely rejected by Islam and remained outside it, yet a certain number of them gained admission and eased the way for the worship of saints and "marabouts"; the belief in a hierarchy of living *walīs*, who exercise divinely conferred powers in this world; and other such elements, which were taken up into Sufi thought.

It is only when we have realized this that we may come to understand a little better why the Muslim theologians formulated and developed their doctrine of the otherness of God in such absolute and uncompromising terms. Their fortress had to be unassailable, for otherwise it could not have withstood the joint pressure of atavistic animism and philosophical pantheism. The danger lay not so much in the outward assaults of Sufi theological pantheism, for they were halfheartedly led and their intellectual equipment was seldom of the best, but from the insidious sapping of the spirit and morale of the defending forces. By their unyielding stand and their forging of rational weapons of defense and offense in spite of the protests and the hindrances offered by the more simple-minded and less clear-sighted believers, they shielded these weaker brethren from the enemy which they so heedlessly ignored and anchored the doctrine of the transcendence of God upon such solid foundations in the Muslim heart and mind that it held fast against all the compromises of the Sufi with the animistic instincts.

Yet there were some paradoxical features in this situation, which are the more deserving of remark because they are also highly relevant to present-day conditions. The theologians who so successfully defended the transcendental doctrines of the Koran against pantheistic aberrations were quite certain of what it was they were defending. But it is doubtful whether more than a few of them ever clearly understood what it was against which they were defending these doctrines or where, exactly, the strength of the attack lay. For them, that is to say, there was no inner tension but only an outer one; they knew only one of the opposing pulls in the religious consciousness, and, standing at that end of the rope, they put all their weight into it. Of the depth and sincerity of their conviction there can be no question. But, if we are justified in holding that there can be no living religion without inner tension, it would seem to follow that their complete victory would have resulted in a disastrous loss of spiritual vitality in Islam. That is what I meant by calling their system a "transcendental mausoleum," and I have al-Ghazāli on my side, at least, for that is precisely the charge which he brought against it.[4]

But we know that their victory was not complete. The Sufi brotherhoods spread ever more widely over the Muslim lands and drove their roots ever more deeply into the soil of social and religious life. Already in the eighth Islamic century (the fourteenth of our reckoning) the violent resistance to Sufism expressed by the fundamentalist Hanbalite, Ibn Taimīya, and his small body of disciples was regarded by the orthodox generally as a mild form of lunacy.[5] During the later centuries the tension relaxed more and more and gave way to something more like an equilibrium. The brotherhoods cared for the personal religious needs of the people and gave full play to their religious emotions but were generally careful to avoid a clash with the orthodox theology. The doctors and theologians, on their side, entered freely into the Sufi orders and there assisted to hold the balance against extreme pantheistic tendencies.

This working agreement reached its climax in the seventeenth and eighteenth centuries in a remarkably harmonious correlation and interaction. I do not agree with those who declare that the vitality of Islam was gradually declining during this period; indeed, as I have already pointed out, it was just at this time that Islam was showing the greatest external activity, and I believe that one of the reasons is to be found precisely in this harmonious inner relation.[6]

This state could be maintained only so long as nothing intervened to tilt the balance. But new factors must inevitably arise from time to time in every living system, since an equilibrium can never be indefinitely sustained. It is commonly believed that—since Islam was (so it is supposed) fast losing its vitality—the new factors were intrusions from without, impulses radiating out from Europe. This is, in fact, quite untrue. The new tensions arose within Islam itself, by the operation of its own forces.

It may, I think, be granted, without taking an unduly pessimistic view of human nature, that if a state of equilibrium in any organism is accompanied by relaxation of tension, the usual consequence is that the organism tends insensibly to lower its standards. We have seen that the spread of Islam in the new territories to the east and south, in Asia and Africa, was largely the work of the Sufi brotherhoods and that the brotherhoods were in many cases tolerant of traditional usages and habits of thought which ran contrary to the strict practice of Islamic unitarianism. The upshot of this was that in the Muslim community as a whole the balance was gradually tilting against the high orthodox doctrine. The ulema were being dragged in the wake of the Sufis, and their resistance was being gradually transferred, so to speak, to a lower level. Theology was beginning to compromise with Sufi doctrine, the citadel was weakening from within. Sooner or later this downhill movement was bound to call out a reaction—bound to call it out, that is, if the Koran remained a living force in the life of the community—and because of the general declension the reaction, when it came, was formulated in more violent and uncompromising terms.

It is significant that this reaction finally emerged in the Arab world, but less significant—as I see the facts at present—that it emerged in Arabia. The movement led by

Muhammad Ibn Abd al-Wahhāb in the middle of the eighteenth century was not, in principle, an Arabian movement. Its inspiration lay in the puritanical Hanbalite school, the school which recognized *ijmāᶜ* only within the narrowest limits and produced Ibn Taimīya and which still, though much reduced in numbers, lived on in the Hijaz, Iraq, and Palestine.[7] Muhammad Ibn Abd al-Wahhāb, in selecting his native central Arabia as the scene of his mission, was (whether consciously or unconsciously) adopting the same course as was taken by the leaders of similar reformist movements both before and after his time. This course was to seek out some region which was out of reach of an organized political authority, where there was, therefore, an open field for the propagation of his teaching and where, if he were successful, he might be able to build up a strong theocratic organization by the aid of warlike tribesmen. It was by such means that the early Shiᶜites and the Berber empires of the Almoravids and the Almohads had gained their first successes; and so, too, Ibn Abd al-Wahhāb achieved his initial purpose by alliance with the house of Suᶜūd in the fastnesses of Nejd.

The results of this first Wahhabi movement were, and still are, far reaching. In its original phase it shocked the conscience of the Muslim community by the violence and intolerance which it displayed not only toward saint-worship but also toward the accepted orthodox rites and schools. By holding them all guilty of infidelity to the pure transcendental ideal and excluding them from the status of true believers, the first Wahhabis repeated the error of the Kharijites (the uncompromising idealists of the first century of Islam), alienated the sympathy and support of the orthodox, and made themselves heretics. Ultimately, therefore, like all fighting minorities who reject any kind of co-operation with more powerful majorities, their opposition was, in a political sense, crushed. But in its ideal aspect, in the challenge which it flung out to the contamina-

tion of pure Islamic monotheism by the infiltration of animistic practices and pantheistic notions, Wahhabism had
a salutary and revitalizing effect, which spread little by
little over the whole Muslim world.

During the greater part of the nineteenth century, however, the revitalizing element in Wahhabism was obscured
by its revolutionary theocratic aspect. It set an example of
revolt against an "apostate" Muslim government; and its
example was the more eagerly followed in other countries
as their Muslim governments fell more and more patently
under European influence and control. At the beginning of
the nineteenth century it inspired the Indian movements
led by Sharī'at Allāh and Sayyid Ahmad against the de-
cadent Mogul sultanate, the Sikhs, and the British. A few
years later, in the middle and second half of the nineteenth
century, the militant and reformist order founded by the
Algerian shaikh, Muhammad Ibn Ali as-Sanūsi, in Cyre-
naica set up a theocratic state in southern Lybia and equa-
torial Africa in protest against the secularist laxity of the
Ottoman Sultans; and the Mahdist brotherhood was
organized by Muhammad Ahmad as the instrument of revolt in the eastern Sudan against Turco-Egyptian rule and
its European agents. Even in such distant regions as Nigeria and Sumatra, Wahhabi influence contributed to the
outbreak of militant movements.

The same revolutionary theocratic impulse underlay
the activity of the famous revivalist, Jamāl ad-Dīn al-
Afghāni (d. 1897), but with a significant change in direction. By this time the current of European infiltration was
swelling to a flood. Jamāl ad-Dīn strove with all his
energies to dam and, if possible, to sweep back the en-
croaching tide by means of the organized power of the
existing Muslim governments. He brought inspiration and
a popular program to the Pan-Islamic movement by restating the bases of the Islamic community in terms of nationalism. But though Pan-Islamism was, on the political

side, aimed against European penetration, it had an internal reforming aspect also. Jamāl ad-Dīn attacked with the same vigor the abuses which he saw within Islam and the evils of the Muslim governments. It was an essential element in his thought that the Muslim peoples should purify themselves from religious errors and compromises, that Muslim scholars should be abreast of modern currents of thought, and that the Muslim state should stand out as the political expression and vehicle of sound koranic orthodoxy.

Although these various attempts at revolutionary political action all ended in failure, when they are looked at from the outside, they had, nonetheless, strong and enduring effects in the religious sphere. They spread the Wahhabi emphasis on pure doctrine and the reassertion of koranic orthodoxy far and wide—not in the sense of preaching and popularizing the narrow tenets of Wahhabism but in the sense of recalling the great body of Muslims, learned and unlearned alike, to a fuller understanding of what Muslim faith demands and of the dangers with which it was menaced. Sir Muhammad Iqbāl has suggested that if Jamāl ad-Dīn's "indefatigable but divided energy could have devoted itself entirely to Islam as a system of human belief and conduct, the world of Islam, intellectually speaking, would have been on a much more solid ground today."[8] If, as he seems to imply by the context of this sentence, he means that Jamāl ad-Dīn was a man who by his "deep insight into the inner meaning of the history of Muslim thought and life" would have been able to "rethink the whole system of Islam," then I confess that I find it difficult to agree with him. The time for "rethinking" was not yet come. The first and most urgent task, and the essential prerequisite for "rethinking the whole system of Islam," was to set Islam back again on its old solid foundations, so that the "new spirit" which Iqbāl postulates should work upon principles clear, precise, and free from alloy of any kind. And Jamāl ad-Dīn's sole published work, *The Refutation of the Materialists*,⁹ does not by any means suggest a man of such intellectual capacity as Iqbāl indicates.

Before a beginning could, in fact, be made with the reformulation of Islamic doctrine, it was necessary to isolate the religious element in the reform movement from the emotional influences of the revolutionary or nationalist program. This was the task taken up and to some extent accomplished by Jamāl ad-Dīn's most influential pupil, the Egyptian shaikh, Muhammad Abduh, in the later period of his active career. The effect of his teaching was to separate the religious issues from the political conflict, so that (even though they might continue to be associated) they were no longer interdependent and each was set free to develop along its own appropriate lines. If he had been able to win more general support for this doctrine, he might indeed have created a revolution in the thought and outlook of the Muslim world. But among the main body of Muslims, whether conservatives or reformers, it has never been fully accepted. The conservatives rejected it—as they rejected almost all Muhammad Abduh's ideas—a priori and on principle; the modernists, who claim to be his followers, did not understand it and, for external reasons, fell back upon Jamāl ad-Dīn's activism. Although Muhammad Abduh's influence remains alive and is continuing to bear fruit in present-day Islam, the immediate outward consequence of his activities was the emergence of a new fundamentalist school calling themselves the "Salafīya," the upholders of the tradition of the fathers of the Islamic church.

Before taking up in fuller detail the legacy of Muhammad Abduh, we must go back for a little to see what was happening in the meantime on the other side. The Wahhabi reformation and its offshoots were not the only symptoms of renewed activity in Islam during the eighteenth and early nineteenth centuries. There was at the same time a marked revival among the Sufi brotherhoods, accompanied both by the expansion of the older orders and by the formation of new orders. In contrast to the orthodox reform movement, however, this revival was less conspicuous in the central Arab countries than among the non-Arab Muslims and in the fringes of Islamic territory.

The mixed Arab and Berber community of Northwest Africa, which had played a most influential part in the medieval Sufi movement, was again well to the fore in the revival. Several new orders were founded during the eighteenth century in Algeria and Morocco, and they developed an intensive missionary activity not only in their home countries but also in the Sahara and West Africa. One of these, the Tījānīya, gained an unenviable reputation by the ruthless military expeditions organized by its adherents in the Negro lands of West Africa, where it clashed with the peaceful missionary propaganda of the old-established Qādiri order. It is fair to remark, however, that these Tījāni conquests (which had been preceded in West Africa by the campaigns of Othmān Danfodio, under Wahhabi influence, in what is now northern Nigeria) are in sharp contrast to the general character of the missionary movements under Sufi leadership. A more typical example is offered by the campaign of revival and conversion carried out in the eastern Sudan in the first half of the nineteenth century by Muhammad Othmān al-Amīr Ghani, the founder of the Amīrghani order—still, in spite of its sufferings during the Mahdist supremacy, the leading order in the eastern Sudan.

Crossing the Red Sea to Kossayr, he made his way inland to the Nile; here, among a Muslim population, his efforts were mainly confined to enrolling members of the order to which he belonged, but in his journey up the river he did not meet with much success until he reached Aswan; from this point up to Dongola, his journey became quite a triumphant progress; the Nubians hastened to join his order, and the royal pomp with which he was surrounded produced an impressive ef-

fect on this people, and at the same time the fame of his miracles attracted to him large numbers of followers. At Dongola Muhammad
ᶜUthman left the valley of the Nile to go to Kordofan, where he made a
long stay, and it was here that his missionary work among unbelievers
began. Many tribes in this country and about Sennaar were still pagan,
and among these the preaching of Muhammad ᶜUthman achieved a
very remarkable success, and he sought to make his influence permanent by contracting several marriages, the issue of which, after his
death in 1853, carried on the work of the order he founded.[10]

There were similar revivalist movements led by the Sufi
orders in India, especially the great Indian Chishti order,
during the early decades of the nineteenth century; and
among the Tatars of Russia and Siberia, notwithstanding
the efforts of the czarist government to promote conversion
to Christianity and its severe laws against the reconversion
of Christians to Islam, an intensive and successful missionary activity was carried on by the orders throughout the
century.

In view of all this revivalist activity, it is not surprising
that, as the original impulse of the Wahhabi movement
died away in the second half of the nineteenth century, reformist and Sufi movements sometimes tended to coalesce.
Several of the reformers had, as we have seen, adopted the
organization of brotherhoods (as-Sanūsi, for example),
and, on the other hand, the great majority of adherents of
the Sufi orders were, in principle at least, orthodox and
exposed to the same internal and external influences. Consequently, the kind of doctrine preached in Bengal by the
anti-Hindu revivalist, Karāmat Ali of Jaunpur (d. 1873),
could quite fairly be described as orthodox, although he
held that the saints possessed powers of intercession and
that it was meritorious to make offerings at their tombs. It
is, I think, a point of some significance in this connection
that Jamāl ad-Dīn was himself a Sufi, and so, too, in his
earliest years was Muhammad Abduh.

This tendency toward a reconciliation of the two wings
of the Islamic community must not, however, be regarded

as a reversion to the state of affairs prior to the Wahhabi puritan revival. If, as I have suggested, the tension between transcendentalism and immanentism is inherent in every living religion, every movement of spiritual revival must embrace both; and the deeper the insight of the leaders, the more likely they are to appreciate both tendencies, or at least to avoid the extremism which stresses the one to the exclusion of the other. A further influence in this direction was the revival of interest in al-Ghazāli, whose great work on the *Revitalization of Religion* had been reintroduced to the Islamic world at the end of the eighteenth century. Jamāl ad-Dīn and Shaikh Muhammad Abduh were both deep students of al-Ghazāli's thought, and the latter, in particular, owed to his study of al-Ghazāli much of the insistence which he laid on the inward and vital character of religion.

Externally also, the two wings were brought together by their common opposition to European control of Muslim lands and their struggle against the pervasive influences of European culture and material civilization, with a hostility sharpened by bitterness at Christian missionary activity and the competition between Christianity and Islam in India, Indonesia, and Africa. It is this factor which more than any other has overshadowed the whole modern revival. One result has been to render any over-all picture of the modernist movements confused and often obscure in detail. Although, as we shall see presently, the conflict between fundamentalist and Sufi has been renewed, it remains subordinate to the need of maintaining as far as possible a united front against Christendom. As has so often been exemplified in the history of Islamic thought and action, external appearances are to a large extent misleading. It is not only the non-Muslim student, either, who finds it difficult to form an assured judgment. The protagonists themselves are often not fully clear in their own minds; not only are they liable to be confused by the interaction of currents, issues, and events, but the dominance of the political issue militates against a serious thinking-out of the problems of religion.

It is time now to return to Muhammad Abduh. After the detailed and masterly analysis of his teachings made by Dr. Charles C. Adams in his study of *Islam and Modernism in Egypt*, I need not attempt to go over this ground again. In a prolific output of writings and lectures, Abduh dealt, of course, with a great variety of topics, some at length and some more cursorily. But the program which he bequeathed to the reform movement can be summed up under four main heads: (1) the purification of Islam from corrupting influences and practices; (2) the reformation of Muslim higher education; (3) the re-formulation of Islamic doctrine in the light of modern thought; and (4) the defense of Islam against European influences and Christian attacks. There is a clear connection between all these objects; but, in view of the actual developments and for purposes of discussion, it will be convenient to treat them separately. I propose, then, in the first instance, to take up each of these topics in turn and to trace the currents of Muslim thought and action in each of these fields, not only in Egypt and the Near East but also, to the best of my information, in India and the other Islamic countries; for these same questions have exercised the minds of Muslims in all parts of the world, sometimes under the direct or indirect influence of Muhammad Abduh and his followers, sometimes independently and on somewhat different lines.

In Muhammad Abduh's own thought the purification of Islam was a wide concept, embracing many features of contemporary thought and practice. But the aspect which found the readiest and most widespread support was the campaign to eradicate the vices and distortions which permeated the religious life of the people. It linked up with the old controversy, which has been the main theme of this chapter, and enjoyed, in consequence, the sympathy of a

large proportion of the orthodox ulema. Even when the
learned were themselves members of the Sufi orders, they
were strongly opposed to the activities of the so-called
"irregular" orders; to the "shaikhs" who lived on the
credulity of the peasants and the workers; to the survivals
of animism, fetishism, and magic in popular beliefs and
practices; and to the cult of "holy men" and the disorders
which accompanied the *maulids*, or popular festivals at
the tombs of noted saints.[11] The lengths to which the ulema
were prepared to go were, however, determined by individual feeling and respect for *ijmāᶜ*. Few would go so far
as to reject the legality of the cult of saints altogether, and
Shaikh Muhammad Abduh himself maintained only that
Muslims are not required to believe in the miracles attributed to saints or in their powers of intercession.[12]

Yet even while Muhammad Abduh was still alive, his
professed followers were beginning to take a sharper line.
In the matter of doctrine he had made a stand against
uncritical acceptance of authority, or *taqlīd*, as it is called
in Islam. This provided, on the one hand, as we shall see
in the next chapter, a sheet anchor for the lay modernist
movement. But in his published work, and especially in
his *Treatise on Unitarian Theology*, he had revived the rationalizing dialectic of the old schoolmen. His theological
followers, led by a Syrian disciple, Shaikh Rashīd Ridā,
continued the process with a characteristic glide toward
extremism. By carrying the rejection of *taqlīd* back beyond
the founders of the schools to the primitive community of
the *salaf*, the "great ancestors," and combining with this
the quasi-rationalism of scholastic logic, but without
Muhammad Abduh's ballast of catholicity, they naturally
gravitated toward the exclusivism and rigidity of the Hanbalite outlook. In their journal called *al-Manār*, "The Light-
house," the influence of the great conciliator al-Ghazāli was
rapidly replaced by that of the fundamentalist, Ibn
Taimīya. As the most downright opponent of the medieval

schoolmen and of Sufi "innovations," Ibn Taimīya supplied exactly the kind of authority and ammunition that
the *Manār* group needed for their campaign.

In the doctrinal aspect, therefore, as in its social program, the Salafīya took on increasingly the character of a
rationalizing puritan movement, while politically its leaders assumed the mantle of Jamāl ad-Dīn al-Afghānī. Since
the *Manār* and its various local offshoots circulated especially among the trading and artisan populations—the
circles in which Sufism had its deepest roots—one of the
main effects of their propaganda was to reopen the old conflict between transcendental unitarianism and Sufism. As
time went on, the tone of their polemic increased in vigor
and asperity; and, although this involved a clash with the
conservative body of Azhar ulema, they found support in
other quarters.[13]

One of these was the revival of Wahhabism in Arabia
and the influence which it acquired among Muslims generally as a result of the prestige of King Abd al-Azīz Ibn
Suᶜūd. We have seen that the original Wahhabi movement,
because of its violently hostile attitude toward the other
orthodox schools, crossed, in fact if not in theory, the line
separating orthodoxy from heresy. But the revived Wahhabi movement, though not outwardly abating its old
claims, showed in practice a greater degree of tolerance.[14]
In the eighteenth century it was a solitary protest in a
corrupt world; in the twentieth it was only the advance
guard of a widespread movement and no longer surrounded by a ring of hostile populations. Since the Wahhabis, too, looked back to Ibn Taimīya as the greatest of
medieval scholars and acknowledged his authority, it was
natural that the Salafīya should show strong sympathies
with their tenets and outlook, to the extent, indeed, that
they have come to be known in some quarters as "Neo-
Wahhabis." But this association again was not likely to
render them more popular with the Azharite fellow-school-

men of the Hanafis, Shāfiᶜis, and Mālikis, who had been deprived of their former status in Mecca since the Wahhabi occupation in 1925.

The *Manār* party were fortified also by the support they received from like-minded groups in other Muslim countries, and especially in Northwest Africa, India, and Indonesia. In Algeria an "Association of Algerian Ulema" was organized to spread their doctrines, in opposition more especially to the "marabouts" and the Sufi orders. The Algerians went even further than the parent-order; in addition to printed and oral propaganda, they set out to revive and multiply the elementary Koran schools in all parts of the country as a means of influencing the rising generation. Their efforts were crowned with remarkable success, considering the obstacles in their way; but, since the death of the founder, Abd al-Hamīd Ben Badīs, in 1940, the future of the association has become uncertain. Similar but smaller groups were active in both French and Spanish Morocco, while, at the other end of the Eastern Hemisphere, in Sumatra and Java, *"Manār*-modernism" injected new life and enthusiasm into Indonesian Islam.[15]

In India the corresponding organization calls itself "Ahl-i Hadīth," "The Followers of the Prophetic Tradition," and has its own journals, schools, and mosques. It is older than the *Manār* group and more radical in its rejection of *ijmāᶜ* and the decisions of the four orthodox schools. The actual relations between the two bodies do not seem to be organized; but the Ahl-i Hadīth, like the Salafīya, direct their preaching with special vigor against the cults of saints and all "innovations" of Hindu or non-Islamic origin.[16]

Another, but less welcome, body of allies in the struggle waged by the reformers against popular superstitions is composed of the rationalists of all shades, moderate or extreme, who desire to see the modernization of Islamic theology and who, in their condemnation of orthodox medievalism, naturally regard popular saint-worship and all related practices with particular abhorrence. Even among those most attached to the traditions of Islam, Western education has powerfully reinforced the aversion to the cult of saints and the Sufi orders. From the modern secular literature of Egypt it would be easy to make a large collection of passages in which the trickery and the deplorable moral influence of the popular shaikhs are pilloried.

In the very first novel published by a modern Egyptian writer, for example, there is introduced one Shaikh Mas'ūd, "one of the notables of the province and of the revered shaikhs of the brotherhoods in it." The author, describing the awed respect and the lavish hospitality with which the Shaikh was received by the peasants, marvels that he should feel no shame at the contrast between his idle and useless life and their life of hard but honest toil:

But what conscience can dwell in the breast of an impostor, who has neither education nor roots and has adopted this kind of cheating as a means of livelihood? What is this Shaikh Mas'ūd but a man who spent ten years within the walls of al-Azhar without learning anything, who then, when he despaired of success and found that his father was unable to give him any more assistance, abandoned learning to those who are capable of it and went out as a homeless vagrant? First of all he dressed himself in a semblance of haircloth, let his hair grow, and lived as a solitary; but when this trade brought him no profit he cleaned himself up a little, put on an Arab headdress, and went about thereafter claiming a kind of universal uncleship and making promises to those unfortunates who believe that (as the popular proverb says) "Whoever has no uncle has the Devil for an uncle."[17]

But, although the orthodox ulema, too, have joined in the hue and cry, it is doubtful whether the results of this campaign have been either deep or beneficial. From time to time it is asserted that the influence of the orders is declining in this or that country, only to be followed by indisputable evidence of their revival. That they have lost their hold on the middle classes is certain. But in the struggle between secularism and religion to fill the place they have vacated, the effectual religious forces are not those of pure intellectual unitarianism. In those chilly altitudes there is no comfort for the average socially minded individual, with his craving for some personal relationship in his worship. The place of the Sufi mysticism has, therefore, been taken either by the new religious clubs and associations or by the cult of the Prophet Muhammad. But among the popular masses, saint-worship and the religious orders seem to have lost, on the whole, little of their hold. No one who has ever seen that mile-long procession of brotherhood lodges with their banners, trudging in the dust after the Holy Carpet on its annual progress through Cairo, can fail to be impressed by the vitality of the forces which they represent. Not for the first time, the *ijmāᶜ* of the people is opposed to the *ijmāᶜ* of the learned.

CHAPTER III

THE PRINCIPLES OF MODERNISM

THE second and third points in the program of reform associated with the writings and activities of Shaikh Muhammad Abduh are the reformation of Muslim higher education and the formulation of Islamic doctrine in terms, if not of modern thought, at least more acceptable to modern men than the outmoded medieval formulation. Ideally, these two points form two aspects of the same activity. They were (and are) the necessary complement to the campaign for the purification of Islam, or, rather, prerequisite to it, since it was only by raising the general level of Islamic education and by reasserting the basic tenets of Islam in clear and compelling language that the corrupting influences, animistic or materialist, could be exposed and uprooted.

The concept of education set out by Jamāl ad-Dīn in his *Refutation of the Materialists* is so general in its terms as to give little indication of his thought. Muhammad Abduh, on the other hand, in rejecting Jamāl ad-Dīn's revolutionary idealism, made it one of his main objects to broaden the basis of education, above all in the Muslim University of al-Azhar. One of his earliest articles, contributed to the newspaper *al-Ahrām* in 1876, while he was still under the direct influence of Jamāl ad-Dīn, asserted the duty of studying not only the classical Arabic works of dogmatic theology, for the defense of the Faith, but also the modern sciences and the history and religion of Europe in order to learn the reasons for the progress of the West.[1] In later years, as the moving spirit of the Administrative Committee for al-Azhar, set up in 1895, he succeeded in introducing useful administrative reforms,[2] but

all his efforts to secure a widening of the curriculum
foundered on the opposition of the ulema. Yet his patient
labors were not entirely fruitless. The influence which he
wielded over the younger men was immense and lived on
after him. That little by little the authorities of al-Azhar
have been moved or compelled to reorganize the teaching
methods and to introduce history, geography, and the elements of the physical sciences into the university is due in
no small measure to the ferment of the ideas which he im-
planted in the minds of the succeeding generation.[3]

It should not surprise us, however, that al-Azhar yields
slowly and reluctantly to the necessity for change and
that such changes as have been made affect the organization of studies rather than their spirit and substance. The
impatience with al-Azhar which is displayed by the
Western-educated classes and the secular nationalists is
easy to understand. But a school with a tradition of nearly
eight hundred years behind it[4] and, still more, a school
which stands throughout the world of Islam as the guardi-
an and (in a certain sense) the authoritative exponent of
Islamic orthodoxy cannot easily trim its sails to every
passing wind. For all that, the reorganization of studies
nine years ago into three faculties—Islamic law, religious
sciences, and Arabic language, each with three grades:
undergraduate, advanced, and specialization—was a far-
from-negligible step in the modernization of method. No
university, of course, can rise above the level of its teachers, and even the encouragement of research in the specialization grades has not yet weakened the grip of tradition
and authority.

Much the same may be said about all those lesser
madrasas, or college-mosques, in other Muslim countries,
in which the methods, subjects, and traditions of orthodox
religious learning have been handed down from past generations. They, like al-Azhar, are slowly yielding to the
pressure of the new world; but, as in al-Azhar, at least an-

other generation must pass before the results of the changes already made can begin to show themselves. To try either to forecast those results at the present time or to deny that further and more fundamental changes can and will be made would be to make an irresponsible leap into prophecy.

Since the earlier reformers were concerned primarily with religious questions, it was natural that they should concentrate on the reform of higher education. This may explain why they gave relatively less attention to what, in the then state of the Muslim world, seems to us to have been so much more necessary—the extension of primary and secondary schooling and the stamping-out of illiteracy. In directing themselves, first and foremost, to the existing religious schools, they were entitled to believe that if these were reformed they would set the tone for education everywhere. It must be remembered that down to the beginning of this century there were no institutions of higher education in Egypt except the college-mosque of al-Azhar and its offshoot, the training college called Dār al-Ulūm. What they had not fully realized was that, in Egypt and in other parts of the Muslim East, education was already split in two; that the systems of primary and secondary education were already divorced from al-Azhar and the religious schools; and that postsecondary education was supplied not by al-Azhar but by foreign universities, in Europe or Beirut.

The reformers did not, of course, entirely neglect the problems of secondary education. They, and still more their successors, were diligent in calling attention to the dangers of sending Muslim boys and girls to foreign and missionary schools; in demanding adequate provision for Muslim religious teaching in all schools; and in pressing for the provision of government schools to replace the foreign schools. They could not foresee that the consequence of extending secondary education would be a demand for the creation of universities of a Western type, which would, at best, compete with al-Azhar and might very well relegate al-Azhar to an inferior position. This is, indeed, what has happened; already Egypt has two modern universities, and al-Azhar has been forced to fight with all the means at its disposal to preserve something like an equality of status with them.

It is important for us to appreciate the width of this rift between religious and secular education in Egypt and its far-reaching consequences. Not only has it ranged school against school and university against university; but it has contributed more than any other single factor to the division in Muslim society, which is to be seen especially in the larger towns, ranging orthodox against "Westernizer" in almost every department of social and intellectual activity, in manner of dress, living, social habits, entertainment, literature, and even speech.

It is the fact of this rift and the necessity of closing it which justifies the rise of modernism. At the same time, it sets the terms of the dilemma into which the reform movement was inexorably forced. On the one hand, in striving toward a modernized formulation of Islamic principles and doctrine, the reformers—like all other reformers before them, in all communities and societies, secular as well as religious—outstripped the great body of the learned, not to speak of the masses. Thus their influence was far greater among educated Muslims outside the ranks of the professional men of religion. I may quote here some sentences that I have written elsewhere of Shaikh Muhammad Abduh:

His real disciples were found among the laymen, more especially the European-educated classes, and that in two directions. In the first place he and his writings formed, and still form, a shield, a support, and a weapon for [the] social and political reformers. . . . . By the authority of his name "they were able to gain acceptance among the people for those of the new principles for which they could not have gained a hearing before." In the second place he bridged, at least temporarily, the widening gap between the traditional learning and the new rationalism introduced from the West, and made it possible for the Muslim graduate of the Western universities to prosecute his studies without being conscious of a fear, or incurring the reproach, that he had abjured his faith. With the removal of this inhibition Muslim Egypt seemed to win a release of energy. . . . . He, more than any other man, gave Egyptian thought a centre of gravity, and created . . . . a literature inspired by definite ideals of progress within an Islamic framework.[5]

But, on the other hand, it should not be assumed, either, that the body of secularly educated Muslims accepted Muhammad Abduh's religious doctrines as their own or that they have stood still in the forty years since his death. In his published works, Shaikh Muhammad Abduh still expressed himself to a great extent in the traditional language of orthodox theology and dialectic; and few but professional theologians could appreciate the points at which he broke with the scholastic structure of dogma elaborated in the Middle Ages. What impressed his lay readers was the spirit in which he approached questions of dogma and practice, and especially his forceful rejection of the traditional teaching that the doctrines of the Koran had been authoritatively expounded once for all by the doctors of the first three centuries of Islam, that their expositions had been confirmed by an irrevocable *ijmāᶜ*, and that no free investigation of the sources could be tolerated.

Islam has condemned blind imitation in matters of belief and the mechanical performance of religious duties. . . . . Islam drew the intellect out of its slumber . . . . and raised its voice against the prejudices of ignorance, declaring that man was not made to be led by the rein but that it was in his nature to guide himself by science and knowledge, the science of the universe and the knowledge of things past. . . . . Islam turns us away from exclusive attachment to the things that come to us from our fathers. . . . . It shows us that the fact of preceding us in point of time constitutes neither a proof of knowledge nor a superiority of mind and intellect, that ancestors and descendants are equal in critical acumen and in natural abilities. . . . . Thus it delivered reason from all its chains, liberated it from the blind imitation that had enslaved it, and restored to it its domain in which it makes its own decision in accordance with its own judgment and wisdom. . . . . Nevertheless, it must humble itself before God alone and stop at the limits set by the Faith; but within these bounds there is no barrier to its activity and there is no limit to the speculations which may be carried on under its aegis.[6]

The effect upon the rising generation of such passages, with their repeated emphasis upon the rights of reason within its own field, was further strengthened by his arguments that there can be no conflict between religion and physical science, that the Koran commands men to engage in scientific studies, and that "our first duty is to endeavour with all our might and main to spread the sciences in our country."[7]

The most encouraging feature in all this for the new Muslim professional classes was that the rejection of authority and the assurance of the harmony between science and religion was issued by one of the highest religious authorities and not (as might have been expected) put forward by the leaders of secular education in the teeth of ecclesiastical opposition. Thus they were both liberated from, and forearmed against, the attempted control of those whom they called the "obscurantists" of al-Azhar.

But the divorce between secular and religious education carried with it the serious consequence that those liberties were interpreted in a manner very different from Muhammad Abduh's interpretation. The graduate of the religious schools was well aware of those "limits set by the Faith" to the exercise of reason; to the secularly educated they were both less substantial and more subjective; and the wider and deeper the new education goes, the greater the divergence becomes. Leaving aside altogether the growth of a pure rationalism which rejects all the claims of religious dogma (and it is noteworthy that, although such a tendency exists, it finds only a very limited expression in Muslim lands) and confining ourselves to the larger class of those who still profess allegiance to the faith of Islam, we should expect the movement of thought to be in some degree parallel to the developments of Western thought in the nineteenth century.

As a basis of comparison and measurement, we cannot do better than take the clear outline drawn by Professor C. C. J. Webb in his Riddell Memorial Lectures on *Religion and the Thought of To-day*.[8] In the eighteenth century, he pointed out, champions and critics alike of Christianity accepted three propositions: (1) that the God whose existence could be demonstrated by rational proofs was a transcendent Being quite distinct from the world which He had created by an exercise of His will; (2) that Christianity stood or fell with the authority of the Scriptures, which claimed to be a revelation of God's will and purpose and therefore (when rightly understood) entirely exempt from error; and (3) that the ultimate sanction of religion was the eventual happiness or unhappiness of the individual in another life.

In the nineteenth century, however, the views of educated men on all these points were revolutionized. In place of the old rational theology, which had been destroyed by Kant, the new defense of religion relied upon the consciousness of the divine to be found in the souls of men; and this tendency to emphasize an immanent rather than a transcendent God was strengthened by the prevailing concept of development or evolution. Second, the application of the same idea of evolution (which in this context has nothing to do with Darwin's theory of natural selection) to social and cultural life assisted the growth of a new conception of history, which was eventually applied also to the books of the Jewish and Christian Scriptures. This conception of history insists that for a real understanding of any system of ideas, it must be placed in relation to what went before and be seen as part of a gradual and continual process of growth. The Scriptures are thus held to reflect in many matters the thought of their own age as distinct from that of ours. "The fact of some statement being included in the Bible does not guarantee its truth or even its religious value, nor does anything which we otherwise judge to be true or right lack something which is needful to make it an object of belief or rule of practice until a Scriptural sanction can be found for it," although "the unequalled value, moral, spiritual and religious, of its general teaching" continues to be accepted by religious minds. Third, the return of European thought since the Renaissance to the Hellenic estimate of civilization as good in itself has weakened men's preoccupation with their future life and induced a certain "double-mindedness" in their outlook; and the attempt to remove this double-mindedness by seeking the religious values within, rather than outside, the world and its civilization harmonized with the general tendency toward immanentism and with the belief in "progress" as the law of human history.

We need not pursue this discussion into the more recent reactions in Christian thought against immanentist theology, since they have no relation to our present subject. The points which I wish to make are that, generally speaking, the orthodox positions in Islam are very closely parallel to the eighteenth-century positions in relation to Christian doctrine and that, during the last hundred years, the extension of secular education in the Muslim countries has exposed educated Muslims to the same influences as have revolutionized Western thought on these religious questions. If like causes produce like results, we should expect to see similar developments in religious thought among Muslims. How far, in fact, is this expectation realized?

In trying to answer this question I shall begin with a brief analysis of the modernist movement, first in Egypt and then in India. We ought also to include developments in Turkey and Persia, both for their intrinsic interest and for purposes of comparison. But the religious aspects of the modern Turkish and Persian revolutions have not yet been adequately studied; and, rather than rely upon the superficial materials and judgments which are all that is at present available, I must reluctantly leave them aside.[9]

It would, I think, be impossible to find any Muslim Arab writer who takes up a position at all comparable with the average nineteenth-century view, as summed up by Professor Webb. One reason that may be suggested for this negative result is the fact that, except for professional men of religion and Muslim propagandists, there are very few Arabs indeed who write on religious questions. In the writings of the ulema, on the other hand, it would be useless to look for anything of the kind, since they, as a class, have remained to a large extent unaffected by the spirit of secular education and of modern Western thought.

It is precisely in this fact that one of the most striking differences between the Christian West and the Islamic world is to be found. Whereas, in the West it is very largely the theologians themselves who are reshaping religious thought in terms of the prevailing philosophical and historical ideas, among Muslim theologians there has been no corresponding activity, except to the very limited extent that we have seen in Shaikh Muhammad Abduh's work. The attitude of the vast majority of the orthodox ulema resembles that of the Roman Catholic hierarchy toward the similar problem in our own civilization. It is a strict and unbending refusal to countenance any kind of truckling to the new philosophies and sciences. For them, these are all nothing but *ahwā*—velleities, caprices, unsubstantial imaginings of the rebellious human mind, or satanic devices to ensnare the heedless and the foolish. A thousand years ago their ancestors met the assault of Greek philosophy in the same spirit and stood their ground. If Islam is a divine revelation, as they believe, history will repeat itself; the forces of materialism, which the Divine Providence in its wisdom has permitted for a time

to tempt and to mislead the sick-hearted and the hypo-
crites, will surely be overcome. Islam needs no apology, no
laborious twisting of the plain meaning of the Koran, no
weak-kneed surrender of its heritage of tradition and law.
At most, where the reformers take up a stand in defense of
the traditional Muslim institutions, there are many conservatives who see no harm in echoing their apologetic,
even when it conflicts in part with the old system of
thought.

It is not to be wondered at that to the generality of the
Muslim ulema the West stands for pure materialism. They
do not know what lies behind all the external manifestations of Western material civilization, and they judge it
mainly by its reflections in Muslim life and Muslim writings—reflections which are often fantastically divorced
from the spirit of Western culture. In spite of the pleadings
of Muhammad Abduh that the ulema should strive with
all their might and main to acquire and to spread knowledge of the sciences, the Azhar type of education still gives
its students only a superficial acquaintance with modern
developments in the realms of science and thought. Moreover, it is only in the last few years that any language
other than Arabic has been introduced into the curriculum. The handicap which this has imposed may be realized from the fact that it is at the present time impossible to produce an adequate Arabic translation of any advanced work of modern science or philosophy. Even if the
effort were made, the result would be unintelligible except
to those readers who could mentally retranslate it into
the Western terms. But it must be allowed that the
philosophical and scientific knowledge of the Azhar graduates, even if it is superficial, is not more superficial than
that of the great majority of the graduates from the
secondary schools and the reading public.

Modernism is, therefore, predominantly a movement of
thought among educated laymen, if we leave aside the

neo-Hanbalite *Manār*-modernists. But how is its theological content to be assessed or defined? It seldom finds
direct expression in books or articles; and, though it may
be reflected in the arguments and polemics of the ulema
against the spread of secularism, we may be sure that, in
the invariable habit of preachers and polemists, they exaggerate, misrepresent, and distort the opinions and activities of which they disapprove. To pin down in definite
terms a movement of ideas so general in its nature is a
difficult and hazardous task. But what is more serious is
the effect among modernists themselves of this unwilling-
ness to think out and to define their positions clearly.
Instead of a broad current of soundly based and rationally
acceptable arguments, modernism, lacking the discipline
of controlled thinking, often loses itself in a maze of subjective impulses and is ever liable to the danger of plunging
headlong over some unseen precipice.

Yet I must venture to make some general statements.
The influence of secular education has done little to dis-
turb at least outward acceptance of the basic theological
doctrines of Islam. In so far as it has helped to discredit
the aberrations and superstitions of popular Sufism, it has
even contributed to strengthening orthodox transcendentalism. Close analysis—much closer and more intimate
than is yet conceivable—would probably reveal, on the
other hand, that orthodox transcendentalism often sur-
vives only as a vague theism, or even deism, though it still
uses the traditional Muslim formulas.

In the second place, the doctrines of relativity and of development or evolution (in the historical, not the biological, sense) are by no means foreign to Muslim thought.
We shall touch on this question again later, in connection
with the Muslim view of history. For the present, it may
be said that the ground was already prepared for the concept of historical development by the Islamic doctrine of a
succession of revelations, each supplementing and more

perfect than the preceding, in harmony with the growing maturity and intelligence of mankind. As against this, however, it went on to assert, with characteristic absolutism, that the Koran was the final and perfect revelation, with the further implication that historical evolution had reached its term.

The Wahhabi reformation, too, with its rejection of medieval and modern "accretions" and "innovations," reopened the door to critical study of the medieval works on tradition and law. For the modernists this has become an indispensable weapon of apologetic, though not (as we shall see) always wielded with discrimination. How far the medieval "science of tradition" has been shaken may be judged from the fact that in 1941 the Council of Ulema of al-Azhar approved a proposal to prepare a new collection of all "sound" traditions and a further collection of the spurious so-called "Israelite" traditions to be found in the medieval commentaries—both of them tasks involving the critical examination of works accepted as authoritative by all the orthodox until recently.

In contrast to the tradition, the Koran itself has remained almost untouched by any breath of evolutionary criticism. Only a few Indian liberals and still fewer Arab socialists have yet ventured to question that it is the literally inspired Word of God and that its every statement is eternally true, right, and valid.

So much for the outward theological position of the modernists—a very different position, it will be admitted, from what might have been expected in the light of Professor Clement Webb's analysis. But, underneath this outward conformity, the secularization of thought and the replacing of an otherworldly by a this-worldly outlook has gone at times very far indeed. It would, however, be absurd to regard secularism as a purely Western importation into the Muslim world. In every developed civilization, including the medieval Islamic civilization, secular-

ism is to be found in a greater or less degree, whether open
or concealed. Indeed, the ulema themselves have contributed to the spread of secularism, for in the Muslim
world it was mainly by the influence of the Sufi orders that
the tendency to worldliness among the educated classes
was counteracted; and in weakening that influence the
ulema have not succeeded in putting any other religious influence in its place, except to the extent that they have co-
operated in the new religious societies, to which reference
will be made shortly.

It was, therefore, into a house already swept bare that
the secularizing influences from the West penetrated,
through Western science, economics, and literature and
through the dissolving effects upon the old social structure
of secular education, of expanding means of communication, of urban industries, and a host of other Western in-
filtrations. But it is remarkable that in the Arab world,
unlike India, there has been little penetration of Western
philosophy. The immanentist tendencies in Western
thought have not been brought consciously into conflict
with the prevailing current of Muslim transcendentalism.
I do not think any Arabs or Egyptians ever read Western
theological works, and the study of Western philosophy in
the Egyptian universities does not go very deep.

Nevertheless, it is impossible for the Muslim who ab-
sorbs a secular education on Western lines to avoid some
overlay of Western thought in his mental activity; and if it
does not take a religious form, it creates an implicit tendency to adopt the values, humanistic or otherwise, that are
manifested in Western civilization and to apply the concept of evolution without regard to Muslim theological
limitations. Western education, that is to say, has fostered
in the Muslim world something of that same double-
mindedness that is to be found in our Western society, even
if the dualism is partly concealed by a profession of orthodoxy. And thereby a new tension has been introduced into

Islamic thought, but a tension of which Muslims in general are not yet fully conscious and whose terms they would find it difficult to define.

We must not, of course, think of all Westernizers as secular minded and antireligious, even if it is true that a great number of the educated neglect the observances of religion. With those who are definitely secularists and who reject the religious claims of Islam altogether, we have nothing to do in these chapters. The larger class of those whom the Koran calls "heedless" would scarcely concern us either, were it not for one problem which they illustrate in Islamic society. It is the ethical problem, familiar in our own society, which arises when belief in eternal reward or punishment after this life has become, if not formally discarded, at least entirely meaningless. In the Christian West the seriousness of this problem is everywhere recognized; in the Muslim East it scarcely seems to have been formulated as yet in specific terms.

Theoretically, the terms of the problem are not quite comparable in the two religions, since Islam rejects any utilitarianism in its ethics.[10] Yet it can scarcely be denied that the sanctions of a future judgment exercised a powerful restraining influence upon the great mass of Muslims; and there have been many indications, in Egypt as well as in Turkey, of the moral breakdown which follows the loss of effective religious belief. The frequent diatribes of the ulema against these manifestations rarely carry conviction, since they generally rely for their effectiveness upon the acceptance of precisely these sanctions and too often include trivial deviations from the traditional code of manners in their catalogue of modern sins. Only the *Manār* group, so far as I know, have made some attempt to restate the principles of Islamic ethics in terms of social values.[11]

I propose, therefore, to limit the term "modernists" to those who do care, and sometimes care deeply, about their religion but who are, in various degrees, offended by the

traditional dogmatics and by the insistence of the conservatives upon the sanctity of the traditional social institutions in the Muslim world. For the majority the issues
in dispute are mainly those relating to the practical duties
and the social institutions of Islam. It is only one or two
exceptional men who raise the argument to a more philosophical level, where the old metaphors in which the doctrines of Islam were expressed (and which are still accepted and believed in by the conservatives) no longer
seem adequate to experience and who therefore reach out
to new metaphors in closer accord with their widened
vision of the universe. In so doing, no doubt, they run the
risk of losing their grasp upon some part of the religious
heritage of Islam, since all religion is in some subtle way
bound up with its metaphors.

But as yet it is only in India, and perhaps Turkey, that
modernists have begun to re-examine the foundations of
belief. Elsewhere the modernist differs from the conservative, theologically, only in building up a Muslim apologetic
on somewhat superficial "modernist" lines, capable of appealing to the superficially "modernist" reader. When we
come to examine the religious content of this apologetic
in the next chapter, we shall find that it often seems to be
directed rather against Christianity than against conservative orthodoxy; but much that, on the face of it, looks like
anti-Christian polemic is, in reality, an apologetic directed
toward Muslim doubters. The object of the apologists is to
prove the divinely inspired origin of the Islamic religion
and way of life, in order to establish and strengthen the
foundations of an ethic which would otherwise stand exposed and helpless before the subtle assaults of secularism. Though we may deplore the hostility to Christianity
which it so often displays, we should, I think, regard with
sympathy the true object of this apologetic. What matters
is sincerity of purpose in endeavoring to counter an over-
whelming evil and to keep alive the spirit of reverence and

the inner moral sense that we call the "voice of conscience."

In our preoccupation with modernism, however, we must be careful not to exaggerate its extent or its importance. The strength and influence of conservative Islam is not to be underrated. In the Arab lands outside Egypt it is everywhere dominant. There is little modernism outside the larger cities in Syria and Iraq or among the Muslims of Northwest Africa. And in Egypt itself the ulema keep a sharp watch on the activities of the modernists, ready to fall upon them as soon as they appear to go beyond the limited range secured for them by Shaikh Muhammad Abduh.

It is, as one would expect, in regard to members of the corps of ulema themselves that their zeal for strict orthodoxy is most fully displayed. When, in 1925, Shaikh Ali Abd ar-Rāziq, one of Muhammad Abduh's disciples, published a treatise advocating the abolition of the caliphate and the separation of civil affairs from the religious code, he was found guilty of unorthodoxy by a unanimous decision of the Court of Ulema of al-Azhar, dismissed, and declared incapable of holding any religious office.[12] In 1930 another shaikh, Muhammad Abu Zaid, published an edition of the Koran with annotations, criticizing the old commentaries and interpreting supernatural references in simple naturalist ways. Although the purpose of the work was to encourage the younger generation to study the Koran, the book was confiscated by the police, and an injunction was secured to prevent the writer from preaching or holding religious meetings.[13]

Lay teachers also have been subjected to similar heresy-hunts, such as the notorious case of Dr. Taha Husain, one of the leading Arabic scholars at the modern University of Cairo, whose destructive criticism of pre-Islamic Arabic poetry roused a storm of reprobation.[14] And many more obscure teachers in Egypt could tell similar stories of pressure brought to bear, often on mere suspicion. In all these activities the Azhar shaikhs have enjoyed the not always welcome support of the *Manār* party, whose virulence has spared no effort to stir up popular feeling against the offenders and to force the sometimes reluctant Azhar and civil authorities to take action against them.

However, although the shaikhs of al-Azhar have assumed the role of guardians of public morals, they are anxious to avoid any suspicion of mere obscurantism from being attached to orthodoxy and even to appear to a certain degree "modern" and "up to date." Thus, on the whole, except for a few extremists, there is remarkably little bitterness in the Arab lands between modernists and conservatives. Together with the external pressures already referred to, the characteristic Islamic spirit of catholicity and comprehension makes for moderation and the avoidance of violence on both sides.

Indeed, it goes further and leads to actual co-operation in one of the most important modern developments—I mean the formation of those religious associations or clubs which have taken the place of the old Sufi brotherhoods among the urban middle classes. The modernist tension itself seeks an outlet in subjective enthusiasm, and this it has found in the new associations, the "Y.M.M.A." (Association of Muslim Youth), the Society of Islamic Guidance, and so on, many of which derive their strength and energy mainly from members of the educated classes and have branches in Syria and Iraq, as well as in most of the towns of Egypt. It is true that these societies sometimes seem to stress outward loyalties rather than inner religion; but, as instruments of modern apologetic and the maintenance of the tradition of worship, they occupy at present a special place in the religious life of the Muslim East.[15]

When we turn to India, the other active center of Islamic thought, we shall find much that resembles what we have already seen in Egypt, but also much that has developed on different lines. India has its own Azhar, the Dār al-Ulūm at Deoband, tied to medieval scholasticism and the tradition, reformist only in so far as it strives to eliminate "innovations" and restore a pure transcendentalism. It has its liberal orthodox reformers of several schools, liberal only to the extent of allowing minor adjustments to meet the pressure of modern conditions. A typical institution is the Nadwat al-Ulema of Lucknow, founded by Muham- mad Shibli, called "Nuʿmāni" (d. 1914). Shibli aimed at introducing literary and historical criticism into Indian Islam, and he tried to face the problems of modern phi- losophy in the light of Muslim thought, although the strict conservatives might accuse him of rationalism. He was, perhaps, the nearest Indian equivalent of Shaikh Muham- mad Abduh, although the impulse which moved him was not so much to work forward from the classical theology to modernism as to work back to liberal orthodoxy, in re- action from what he regarded as an exaggerated secular modernism. The professedly reformist but fundamentalist *Manār* movement seems to be paralleled in India not only by the Ahl-i Hadīth, but also by the *Sīrat* movement, of whose activities I know only from the scanty references to it in Mr. Wilfred Smith's book.

Alongside these, however, there are trends of thought in India which go much further than anything in the Near East. For this there are several reasons. Higher education of a Western type has been established in India for a much longer period of time and over a much wider range of popu- lation than in Egypt or Syria. This has brought into exist- ence a large body of educated Muslim laymen, who may not be proportionately much more numerous than the educated classes in the Near East but are numerically greater, and more of whom hold high positions as leaders and teachers in their community. Their independent status and relative freedom from government interference liberates them from the vexatious consequences of heresy-hunts and the censorship of the religious authorities and encourages them to express their own philosophy of religion with greater freedom. The more advanced modernism of India is thus, in the main, a lay movement led by officials, lawyers, propertied men, and university teachers, in opposition to the conservative ulema and Sufi orders.

This fact supplies a prima facie justification for Mr. Smith's treatment of modern Islamic movements in India in terms of their social and economic setting, so that (to quote his publisher's words) "the class content of religious ideology is constantly brought to light." Passing his facts through a fine sieve of doctrinal analysis, sharpened by the dogmatism of our younger socialists, it is not surprising that he finds little good grain and a vast quantity of chaff.

But though I cannot follow him entirely in his "devastating criticism," the student who passes from the Near East to India cannot but be conscious of a more marked political content in its religious movements. That they should include a definable social or social-economic aspect is not to deny the sincerity of their leaders or of the mass of Indian Muslims. In contrast with the Arab lands, Islam in India can never free itself from its setting over against the vast Hindu majority; and this, of necessity, forces social and political issues into the context of religious life. Moreover, the range of social and racial differences within the Muslim community suggests of itself a society in which religious attitudes are closely related to social backgrounds. And, finally, since the social background of the educated classes has been strongly affected by English education and ideas within a framework of British government, it is inevitable that modern Indian "religious ideologies" should be to a greater or less degree conditioned by attraction to or repulsion from English ideas or British government.

Since the essential principle of modernism is the Protestant principle of the right of free examination of the sources

and the application of modern thought to their interpretation, irrespective of the constructions of early doctors and
legists, it follows that modernist movements are generally
personal and individual and less patient of organization
than movements based on tradition. The most remarkable
feature of the first Indian modernist movement, led by Sir
Sayyid Ahmad Khān (d. 1898), was its organized character. This it owed mainly to the foundation of a college
at Aligarh in 1875, now (since 1920) the Muslim University, with the object of combining religious education with
modern scientific studies. From its founder's insistence
that the proof of the truth of Islam was its "conformity to
nature," his school gained the name of *nechari*, and under
that name earned the violent denunciation of Jamāl ad-
Dīn al-Afghāni, whose work, published as *The Refutation
of the Materialists*, was, in fact, directed primarily against
it. He wrote:

> *Nechariya* is the root of corruption, the source of uncountable evils
> and the ruin of the country. . . . . The *Necharis* present themselves be-
> fore the eyes of fools as the standard-bearers of science, but only give a
> wider range to treachery. They are deluded by catchwords, call them-
> selves guides and leaders, when they stand in the lowest grades of igno-
> rance and lack of intelligence.

In spite of these bitter attacks, however, echoed by the
conservative ulema, the Aligarh school flourished and
formed the root from which most of the later developments of Indian modernism stem, directly or indirectly.

The principle of "conformity to nature" in Sir Sayyid
Ahmad Khān's view really meant little more than a
tendency toward rationalism and rejection of the miraculous. The phrase caught on, however; and, when pushed
to extremes and combined with a smattering of physical
science, it could and did produce many extravagances and
absurdities. We can neglect most of these; but I may quote
one example, taken not from an Indian work but from an
Iraqi Arab poet, Jamīl Sidqi az-Zahāwi. In a fantasy pub-

lished in 1931 under the title of *Revolution in Hell*, he begins by relating his examination after death by the two
angels, Munkar and Nakīr, who, according to Muslim belief, visit and question the souls of the dead in the grave.
The poet faces his accusers boldly, as the following passage shows:

> The angel asked "What is God's Being?" I replied. . . .
> "Of the Being of God I know nothing, for a veil hangs over it.
> All that I know is this, that God lives and passes not away.
> Everything existent has but one God that perishes not, and
>   that is the Ether.
> From it streams out all life, and to it life returns after
>   extinction.
> Ether and God—there is no difference but in expression,
>   if understanding guides one aright."[16]

In the generation after Sir Sayyid Ahmad Khān, several
scholars, of whom the Shiʿite, Sayyid Amīr Ali, was the
foremost, worked out a new Muslim liberal apologetic and
ideology, which has replaced for thousands (if not millions)
of Muslims the traditional presentation—and that not
only in India but throughout the Muslim world. We shall
examine this apologetic in some detail later. But after this
achievement Indian modernism seemed to have had no
center of gravity. The social and political conflicts that
have distracted India since the beginning of this century
had their reactions also upon the religious outlook of the
Muslim community and created new groupings within it.
Of its various leaders, the most outstanding in intellectual
life between 1910 and his death in 1938 was Sir Muhammad Iqbāl, poet and philosopher; but Iqbāl himself, by the
contradictions and confusions in his thought, only accentuated the instability and inner conflict of ideas.

Iqbāl is perhaps the most interesting figure in the whole
modern Islamic community, but also intellectually the
most elusive. Inspired in early life with a passion for philosophy, he studied in England and Germany, and, on return-
ing to India, he took up the profession of law for the sake of

the independence which it gave him. From 1915 onward he expressed his thought in a series of poetical works, which gained the enthusiastic applause of the younger Muslim intellectuals; and in 1928 he put together a systematic philosophical exposition in his *Six Lectures on the Reconstruction of Religious Thought in Islam.* These present the first (and so far the only) thoroughgoing attempt to restate the theology of Islam in modern immanentist terms. We shall analyze them in the next chapter; here I need only say that, although, in order to gain a wider audience, he wrote most of his poetry in Persian and his lectures in English, I have seen no indications that they have exerted any influence anywhere outside India.

His poems appear to me to be full of strange contradictions, although his Indian followers have tried to organize them into some sort of system.[17] His most insistent doctrine is the necessity for Muslims to throw off the lethargy and the inhibitions of the past, to develop and enlarge their personalities, to prepare for the emergence of the Superman; but, alongside this, he preached by turns a kind of vague socialism and an uncompromising obedience to the social ideals of Islam:

> O thou that art emancipated from the old Custom,
> Adorn thy feet once more with the same fine silver chain!
> Do not complain of the hardness of the Law,
> Do not transgress the statutes of Muhammad![18]

A keen student and follower of Western philosophy, he exhorted Muslims to acquire the science of the West and, almost in the same breath, condemned all Western organizations and institutions as degrading shams. Nationalism and all its works he lashed with scorn; but he wrote the poem which has become the national hymn of the Muslims of India, and he gave the support of his voice and pen to the Pakistan project. And behind all this, and almost in spite of himself, he was inescapably entangled in the net of Sufi thought.

Perhaps the right way to look at Iqbāl is to see in him one who reflected and put into vivid words the diverse currents of ideas that were agitating the minds of Indian Muslims. His sensitive poetic temperament mirrored all that impinged upon it—the backward-looking romanticism of the liberals, the socialist leanings of the younger intellectuals, the longing of the militant Muslim Leaguers for a strong leader to restore the political power of Islam. Every Indian Muslim, dissatisfied with the state of things—religious, social, or political—could and did find in Iqbāl a sympathizer with his troubles and his aspirations and an adviser who bade him seek the way out by self-expression. No wonder there is an "Iqbāl Society" in Lahore and that, since his death, books and articles have poured from Indians pens on Iqbāl's theory of this, that, and the other thing. But what Iqbāl's theories do lead to, in fact, we shall see in due course.

Besides the bewildering profusion of modernist argument and speculation, of orthodox conservatism, Muslim socialism, and the fundamentally nonreligious bigotry of the later reactionary movements (which use Islam only as a political and communal symbol), India has produced also the only successful new sect in Islam. The Ahmadīya movement started as a liberal and pacifist reform movement, offering the attraction of a fresh start to those who had lost faith in the old Islam. The founder, Mirza Ghulām Ahmad, claimed to be not only the Mahdi of Islam and the Messiah of the Christians but also an avatar of Krishna. After his death in 1908 the more liberal elements split off and gradually threw over all that distinguished them from the ordinary liberal Muslims, including their former prophet. By their energetic missionary activity, not so much in India as in England, America, and South, East, and West Africa, these "Lahore Ahmadis" have even earned some merit in orthodox eyes, although strict conservatives remain suspicious both of their dubious origins and of their liberalism.[19]

The original, or Qādiāni, Ahmadis also engage in missionary work in England and America, as well as in India. Each branch has a mosque in the suburbs of London and hospitably entertains not only Indians but also Arab, Persian, Afghan, and other Muslims, even including Wahhabis. But in India the Qādiāni Ahmadīya remains an entirely separate community, with its own mosques, schools, and courts and its own doctrinal authority, the *khalīfa* of the founder. From time to time conflicts have flared up between the Ahmadīya and the Muslims, and some Ahmadi missionaries have even been killed in Afghanistan. But, on the whole, the Ahmadīya are an unimportant element in Indian Islam and only slightly more important as carriers of the liberal interpretation of Islam into the more backward parts of Muslim Africa.

CHAPTER IV

MODERNIST RELIGION

THE fourth point in the modernist program we defined as the defense of Islam against European influences and Christian attacks. The first of these two aims may seem paradoxical. Modernism itself is largely a product of European influences, and sometimes, as we have seen, they may go very deep indeed. The conservatives are well aware of the apparent inconsistency, and it adds to the suspicion with which they regard all modernist activities, even when these are directed to the defense of Islam.[1]

Yet among modernists, as distinct from secularists, the inconsistency is felt to be no more than an apparent one. Whether consciously or not, I think most modernists would meet the charge in some such manner as this: "Modern Western thought is not a single homogeneous stream, which every Muslim must regard as tainted at its source. It is a confluence of many streams, often conflicting with one another. Some of these currents are purely rationalist, deriving from abstract principles whose validity we do not recognize. Others are religious in an exclusively Christian sense, deriving from doctrines which we, as Muslims, reject. But some are the product of pure thought, working outward or inductively from premises which have been experimentally verified and which in no way conflict with the teaching of the Koran, even if the medieval theologians may sometimes have thought differently. It is a duty which is expressly laid upon us, as Muslims, by the Koran to study these new manifestations of thought, to show how they are assumed or prefigured by the Koran, to relate them to the foundations of Muslim belief, and by their aid (rather than by the aid of a medieval apologetic which is no longer adequate) to prove the falsity of the rationalist and the Christian concepts, and so to prevent these two currents of thought from undermining our Faith. Unless we make this effort, the whole of Muslim culture will be swept under by the unresisted tide of Western materialism, whose insidiousness our religious leaders simply do not realize."

In the preceding chapter, I indicated in a general way the frontiers and limitations of most modernist apologetic —limitations which we may call "self-imposed," in a sense. But now, as we come to grips with specific modernist positions, we are confronted at the outset with a much more fundamental weakness. However much we may sympathize with the objectives of the reformers and with their efforts to loosen the grip of the dead hand, it has to be admitted that most of these essays in modernism surprise and sometimes shock us by their methods of argument and treatment of facts. We feel a strain somewhere, a dislocation between the outward argument and the inner train of reasoning. We are all of us familiar with books in our own language which leave us with the feeling that either the author is incapable of handling his materials or his treatment of them is vitiated by writing to a predetermined conclusion. That we should have something of the same feeling about these modernist writings is only natural, when we reflect that modernism involves a revolution in the very concept of knowledge itself.

There is a deeply rooted conflict between medieval and modern ideas of the nature of knowledge. The old Islamic view of knowledge was not a reaching-out to the unknown but a mechanical process of amassing the "known." The known was not conceived of as changing and expanding but as "given" and eternal. Not everybody, of course, could possess all knowledge, but there was at least a fixed sum of knowledge, most of which was in the possession of some persons or other.

This had three important consequences. First, knowledge was not a dynamic element in thought but a solid and immobile mass. Hence in matters of dogma it led to a fundamentalism which crushed independent intellectual activity under the dull weight of authority and eventually destroyed the rich and varied harvest garnered by the philosophical and scientific curiosity of medieval Muslim scholars. The second consequence was that nothing in the accepted scheme of knowledge could be discarded as antiquated, superseded, or disproved; and, conversely, nothing could be regarded as true knowledge unless it was in harmony with what was generally accepted. It was this concept of knowledge as a closed circle, probably, which contributed more than any other factor to the conviction expressed by Western nineteenth-century scholars that Islam could have no future because it displayed no capacity of adaptation to new ideas. Third, the process by which knowledge was acquired was not by analysis, induction, and experiment but by the simple amassing of what already existed or, at most, by deductive reasoning from accepted axioms.

The modernists and reformers have shown that Islam need not remain a petrified system, to be regarded as a mere incumbrance to the progress of thought, and that the old theological limitations of the frontiers of knowledge can be set aside. But the grip of the traditional concept is not so easily shaken off. It is, indeed, perpetuated by the mechanical system of book learning rather than education, which is imposed on pupils in primary and secondary schools and which affects even the universities in most Muslim countries. For the great majority of the educated classes, knowledge is still what one knows rather than what one has yet to learn; it is something to be sought and found in books rather than by free inquiry and at the cost of both physical and mental effort. It has no dynamic quality; it lacks power because it is still inorganic, compartmented, and atomistic. It is still dominated by the idea of authority; and if Western "authorities" are now recognized alongside Muslim "authorities," the result is only to create a confusion of thought, made all the worse by the fact that for all but a few the means of testing their authorities (whether Western or Eastern) and of distinguishing their relative value and reliability do not exist. Because of the lack of intellectual standards, there is no check upon credulity.

The effects of this confusion are reinforced by the influence of the other current of religious thought in Islam. If the orthodox pushed a narrow and literalist conception of knowledge to excessive lengths, the mystics, on the other hand, allowed an equally excessive liberty to pure intuition. Now, however great the value that we may set on the intuitive experience in religion, it is nevertheless true that intuitive thought is rarely associated with precision, whether of content or of expression. And if we bear in mind the atomistic, discrete character of the Arab imagination, which we discussed in the first chapter, we shall not be surprised to find Muslim religious thought on its mystical side characterized by a subjective selectivity, an appositional series of individual points, rarely synthesized and always resistant to analytical treatment. Objective analytical "knowledge" was indeed scorned by the mystics as a positive obstacle to the attainment of spiritual experience of reality.

Ultimately, it seems to me, both systems produced the same attitude to whatever lay outside their own closed circles. It was simply brushed aside, in the one case by elaborate argument and in the other by excluding it from vision. Whatever conflicted with the established orthodox doctrine—even if it were plainly asserted in the Koran—was sidetracked; whatever disturbed the subjective idealism of the mystic was declared to be mere illusion.

That is, of course, an attitude with which we are quite

familiar among ourselves. It is the attitude of the partisan everywhere and on every issue, in party politics, in the press, in clubs and debating societies, in private life. We too easily forget how recent and how limited is the spread of the dispassionate examination of facts, which is an application not so much of scientific technique as of the scientific temper to the data of experience. We too seldom remind ourselves not only how few there are who can apply it at all to any field of experience but how seldom those few apply it in all fields of experience—how often, in fact, no matter how judicial we are in historical or literary research, we allow our feelings to run away with us on political or emotional issues.

How much more allowance, then, must we make for the Muslim modernist! Consider how recent has been the introduction of analytic method into the thought of the Muslim world, how difficult it is to overthrow the age-long domination of atomism and authority. Our world has had four centuries in which to adapt itself—how insecurely still—to this revolution in the concept of knowledge, and it cannot be carried through in one or two generations. The new methods have been, in a sense, superimposed from without; they do not spring from interior habit slowly and gradually built up by generations who have lived through the evolution of the new ways of thinking. What is transmitted by mere contact is always superficial. But it need not remain so. It would be premature to regard the incongruity that we find in modernist writings, this rather awkward superimposing of an external analytic method on a traditional atomistic substructure of thought, as fatally determined by the thought-processes of the Muslim mind. What we are seeing today is only a beginning, and we do not laugh at George Stephenson's locomotives because they could not haul the Twentieth Century Limited.

But, even though we have no right to regard the strain as anything more than a feature of a period of transition, it does produce some undeniable and serious weaknesses in the methods of modernist argument and the tendencies of modernist thought. We must, however, remember also that we are concerned here with apologetic, and apologetic is partisan by its very nature. Whatever the outward profession of the apologist may be, he sets out to defend and to prove the truth of what he is already convinced is the truth. The Muslim apologist therefore sets out with the conviction that the Koran is the literally inspired Word of God and that Christianity is perverted and false. It would be absurd to expect him to doubt either of these propositions. Not only can he not conceive that any Muslim should doubt them and yet remain a Muslim; he cannot even conceive that a Christian should reject the literal inspiration of the Bible and see good in Islam and yet remain a Christian. It is, indeed, one of the pathetic illusions of the Muslim controversialist that a Christian Unitarian is already halfway toward becoming a Muslim.

What interests us, then, in modern Muslim apologetic is not the fact that it is apologetic but the methods of argument which it employs. I have already pointed out that this apologetic is primarily directed toward other Muslims in order to maintain their inner loyalty to Islam; and it is for the literature directed to this end that I shall reserve the word "apologetic." The literature which is directed primarily against Christianity and against the attacks of Christian missionaries I shall call "controversial." But, in fact, I propose to say very little indeed about controversial Muslim writings. It is obvious that they will display the same qualities as Muslim apologetic, only sharpened, exaggerated, and to some extent coarsened; and it adds nothing to our knowledge of Muslim modernism that Muslim controversialists—like other controversialists—can sometimes sink pretty low.

To what kind of public is the modernist apologetic directed? First, of course, to the reading public, that minority of Muslim men who have had a secondary or advanced primary schooling. The illiterate Muslim, the villager, is in no danger yet of losing his faith, and, even if he were, the educated town-bred modernist would have no word to meet his needs. His spiritual life is cared for by the Sufi brotherhoods, regular or irregular, by the imam of the local mosque, or by the itinerant revivalist preacher. So far as modernist ideas reach him, they are filtered through some such medium.

Beyond that, the modernist apologetic is directed to the young men everywhere—to college students, to the middle classes of every degree, to the artisans. These are the classes whose faith and loyalty are most liable to be undermined, whether by the influences of Western education or by the mechanization of modern life or by propaganda of various kinds—missionary, rationalist, or Communist. The danger is by no means exaggerated; and, were it not for this apologetic, it is certain that the proportion of atheists, apostates, and merely nominal Muslims would be much higher than it actually is.

Since Islam is not only a body of religious doctrine but also a way of life with a long tradition behind it, modernist apologetic extends to the whole range of Islamic doctrines and institutions, ethics, and rituals and also to the Islamic past. In some circumstances, indeed, the defense of the institutions and the history calls for the greater effort, because they are the more open to attack both from without and from within. In the present chapter, however, we shall confine ourselves to matters of doctrine, leaving the questions relating to institutions and history to the two following chapters.

Modernism is primarily a function of Western liberalism. It is only to be expected, in consequence, that the general tendency of modernists would be to interpret Islam in terms of liberal humanitarian ideas and values. In the first stage they contended that Islam was not opposed to these ideas; but they soon went on to claim that Islam was the embodiment of them in their highest and most perfect form. In the development of this argument the influence of Christian missionary propaganda played a leading part, to the extent often of determining the particular emphasis which was laid on this or that doctrine or practice. Missionaries have often claimed, and more often complained, that the reformers were simply taking over Christian ideas and values and constructing an entirely new "Christianized" Islam. But, as Mr. Wilfred Smith has very justly pointed out,

that part which they took was not the specifically "Christian" part but the liberal-humanitarian-bourgeois part, the values of nineteenth-century Europe. These values were indeed a real part of Christianity then—just as they are a real part of Islam now. They were not inherent in either religion in its feudal days, neither in mediaeval Christianity, nor in eighteenth-century Indian Islam. It was this last fact that the missionaries, with much biting antagonism, were pointing out. They forgot that there had been societies in which Christianity also had not had a reasonable theology, a "this-worldly" attitude and criterion, a belief in progress, science, and culture, an ethics based on principles rather than a code, a stress on the personality of its founder rather than on his function, an acquiescence in capitalist interest, a feminist programme—and so on. If one had pointed out those societies to the missionaries, they would no doubt have answered that the religion prevalent therein was not "real" Christianity—just as the modern Muslim asserts that early nineteenth-century Islam or modern village Islam is not the "real" Islam, or the modern missionary says that the new Westernized religion of the Aligarh School is not ' really" Islam.[2]

Since both Indian and Egyptian modernism are grafts of the same kind on the same orthodox trunk, the leading ideas of the liberal apologetic in India (which have been very fully and acutely analyzed by Mr. Smith) are practically the same as those which underlie, if they are not actually asserted in, the writings of the Arab Muslim modernists. Indeed, the works of the Indian Sayyid Amīr Ali, especially his *Spirit of Islam*, although written by a Shiʿite and published in English, occupy even in Egypt a leading place among the classics of modernism; and they have furnished materials and arguments for a vast number of articles, pamphlets, lectures, and books. Most of the writers may quite possibly have no direct acquaintance with his books and may be totally unaware of the source of their arguments. But he did more than any other to give a concrete, substantial, and rounded-off presentation of the new liberal conception of Islam. There can be no dispute that this conception has gained the unquestioning or enthusiastic acceptance of those educated Muslims who were vaguely repelled by the conservative presentation and acutely disturbed by conservative insistence upon the final and mandatory character of the traditional institutions of Islam. It has to that extent been successful in attaining its object and, even more strikingly, in moving the conservative ulema to accept and support some of the positions which it has taken up.

But here again we meet a paradox. Just as it was in the Middle Ages, so now the great majority of the conservative theologians know what it is they are defending but do not know (or know only through the distorting glass of modernist apologetic) what they are defending it against. On the other hand, the average middle-class apologist does not really know the Islam which he claims to be defending, and he defends, instead, an imaginative reconstruction on liberal lines which he passionately believes to be the genuine teaching of the Prophet Muhammad. Hence neither party can really "rethink" the religious content of Islam in any profound sense. I have already pointed out that Islam today suffers from the absence of anything comparable to that process of restating the fundamental positions of Christianity by the labors of generations of skilled theologians. And that weakness is accentuated by the fact that even the conservatives know (although they would not admit it) that the medieval theological structure is in ruins.

On the religious plane, then, the new apologetic leaves

aside the fundamental questions and concentrates, in the main, on two subjects: the perfection of the Koran and the personality of Muhammad. Both of these are old and familiar themes in Islam, and modern writers are thus elaborating upon an extensive literature which goes back to the early centuries. What is new is, first, the special emphasis laid upon them and, second, the directions in which the old positions have been extended and elaborated.

The incomparability of the Koran was a cardinal doctrine of Islam from its earliest beginnings. The authenticity of its text (in spite of numerous variant readings) has often been contrasted with the corruptions of the Jewish and Christian Scriptures and adduced as evidence of divine care for its preservation. But for the present generation of Muslims more is needed than that. It has to be shown that nothing in it is false or antiquated, that neither modern scientific nor modern historical thought has affected its authority as a full and final exposition of the universe—otherwise its claim to be regarded as the literal Word of God falls to the ground. What is demanded is essentially a reinterpretation, and one that, on the whole, stresses its material rather than its spiritual truth.

This reinterpretation takes many forms. One of the crudest is to read into koranic texts what is regarded as modern scientific thought, by interpreting, for example, *jinn* as "microbes." I do not wholly share the common tendency to jeer at all this quasi-scientific rationalism. It is no more ridiculous than the attempts of pastors among ourselves a few years ago to "reconcile" the story of Genesis with geology or the still more frequent attempts to present the truths of religion in terms of popular science. The educated Muslim takes the same view of all this as we do, and it is probably no more than a passing phase of apologetic which has served its purpose for a time.[3]

What is much more serious is the discarding of almost

the whole medieval apparatus of interpretation. That remarkable structure had been built up with immense erudition out of the tradition of Medina, the principles of the legal schools, and the elucidation of the historical passages from such sources as were available, including the Jewish Scriptures. But its literalism, on the one hand (especially in relation to the descriptions of paradise and hell), and its free introduction of the miraculous, on the other, are distasteful to modern liberalism. The tradition as a whole, as we shall see when we come to deal with the person of Muhammad, is treated by modernists with scant respect when it runs counter to their ideas, and European scholarship has itself furnished them with the means to discredit it. Thus they feel themselves free to interpret allegorically what they choose and to throw over the miraculous stories which pious imagination elaborated out of koranic verses.

Not only the modernists, however, but also the stricter orthodox can be found adopting the same method, though not so much, perhaps, in regard to the elements rejected by the modernists as in regard to the old historical interpretations, for they have realized that it is, after all, the historical criticism which carries the most dangerous threat to the traditional orthodox view of the Koran, and they have sought to parry the danger by rejecting outright the medieval expansions of koranic narratives and branding them as *Isrāʾīliyāt*, "Jewish legends." For example, in the thirty-eighth chapter of the Koran, there is told a story about David which is obviously based on Nathan's parable of the ewe lamb in II Samuel, chapter 12. The medieval commentators, recognizing this, supplemented the koranic narrative from the Old Testament sources. But this involved introducing the story of Bathsheba, which does not appear in the Koran, although it is stated that David repented and sought forgiveness of his Lord. For later Muslim orthodoxy, however, the sinlessness of the Prophets (David being regarded as a Prophet) became an article of faith. So a recent popular expositor deals with the passage on the following lines:

The stories told in the Koran about men of the past are intended for warning and example, not as biography, history, or entertainment. But many persons were not content to accept them simply as homiletic and proceeded to pad them out with details which were often at variance with their original purpose. Certain commentators caught the infection and gave currency to these stories, the source of which has been traced to imperfectly converted Jews or Christians or to heretics who sought to deceive the Muslims and to sow doubts and dissensions among them. Then, having cleared the board, the expositor goes on to expand the story himself on purely imaginative lines and ends by reaffirming the sinlessness of the Prophets and particularly of David, "whose rank and position were such that it is contrary to reason that he should yield to his lusts and commit those abominations which the storytellers assert."[4]

But it is the second feature of modern Islam—the concentration of religious feeling upon the person of Muhammad—that gives it its characteristic ethos, the more so that this is not confined to modernists but is shared by practically all Muslims. It is true that veneration of Muhammad has always been an integral element of Islam. It is enshrined in the Kalima, the basic confession of faith: "There is but one God and Muhammad is His Prophet." Among the Sufis especially there was a cult of Muhammad, which would have contrasted oddly with their pursuit of absorption in the Divine Essence had the two not been harmonized by a doctrine with recognizably Gnostic affinities.[5] But the ecstatic Sufi hymns to the Prophet find echoes also among the orthodox ulema, and it was only the out-and-out transcendentalists who realized the dangers of this lavishing of religious emotion on the person of the Prophet. The early Wahhabis, for instance, classed it in the same category of "innovations" as saint-worship and strongly asserted that Muhammad was but a man.

Two factors in particular have contributed to heighten this *mystique* of the Prophet. It appears to me that Mr. Wilfred Smith is altogether too obsessed with his class-ideology when he picks on the individualism of capitalist society to substantiate his thesis that "liberal religion is more interested in a person than it is in God." As we have just seen, the *mystique* was already there in preliberal Islam. The fundamental reason, I would suggest, is the re-assertion of the transcendental doctrine within Islam in the nineteenth century and its success in discrediting (if not in suppressing) the emotional outlet afforded by Sufi mysticism. The religious imagination craves some symbol on which to lavish the human instincts of love and trust, and not least among peoples so sensitive and of such vivid emotions as most of the Muslim peoples are. It was these instincts, in reaction against the attempt to confine them within the bounds of a rigid theological system, which sought and found an outlet in the cult of Muhammad "as a companion, who can be relied upon at all times for friend-ship, sympathy and stimulation, and also upon whom friendship and devotion can be bestowed."[6] Together with this personal factor, too, a cult of this kind is peculiarly congenial to the group-spirit, which is fostered by the new religious associations and clubs.

The second factor is also a reaction, this time to Chris-tian aspersions on the character of Muhammad. We need not go back to the medieval legends so judiciously summed up by Professor Samuel C. Chew in *The Crescent and the Rose*, although their influence has still to be reckoned with on both sides. More particularly it was due to the massive assault of Christian missionaries, ruthlessly pressed home in the belief that to contrast the persons of Jesus and Muhammad was the most effective weapon to their hand in their conflict with Islam. Against this assault the orthodox defense proved inadequate, because the ulema could not see where the shoe pinched. Their presentation of the Prophet was soundly based on the historical records; but, in presenting him in all the medieval amplitude of the traditional biographies and seeing no need of apology, they failed to take into account the changing ethical outlook of the new Muslim intellectuals and middle classes. At this point the modernists stepped in and supplied a new image of Muhammad, by which the Christian attack was parried and the defense even turned into an offensive.

Of this new image I need not give a detailed description. It takes, one by one, all the cardinal virtues and presents Muhammad as embodying them in the highest degree. Not only is he made the exemplar of charity, purity, truth, and all the rest, but the newer European ideologies provide a pedestal on which to exalt his manliness, his qualities of insight and leadership, and his revolutionary vigor. The method is the same as in the reinterpretation of the Koran, only applied now to the tradition. Out of that incredibly vast storehouse of anecdote, the modern apologist selects whatever suits his immediate purpose, sweeping aside the old classical science of tradition with its careful controls (however defective they may have been) and substituting no control at all but a purely subjective appreciation. Whatever is in contradiction with his ideas he either discards without more ado or else attempts to discredit by the bare assertion that it is a forgery, put into circulation by secret enemies to Islam or by sycophants of the Umayyad caliphs, who have become convenient whipping-boys or scapegoats for everything that the modernist does not like.

Here again the conservatives have accepted either wholly or in part the new view of the Prophet. Missionaries might refer to it scornfully as "Muhammad-cum-lavender-water";[7] for Muslims it was emotionally, ethical-

ly, and intellectually satisfying. To quote Mr. Smith
again:

> The Muslim who accepted his religion from these [modernist] writings might hold his head high, even when confronting Western Europe. His religion, point by point, is proved the finest in the world—judged by the most modern standards. The Prophet whom he adores is the supreme character of all history. The Muslim might well be proud, and confident. The spirit of his religion, he found, is the highest liberal ideals, put here in contemporary and in glowing terms.[8]

But it is none the less true that the liberal modernists
have achieved this result at a serious cost. Not only have
they discarded or distorted vital elements in the personality of Muhammad (thereby, in my opinion, inflicting a
grave injury upon the historical structure of Islam), but,
by their disregard of all objective standards of investigation and of historical truth, they have debauched the intellectual insight and integrity of their fellow-Muslims. And,
in the second place, by substituting a personal cult for a
reasoned faith, they have weakened, and possibly, indeed,
undermined, the foundations upon which not only Islam
but every religion with any pretensions to universality and
moral stability must stand. They have heightened the intensity of Muslim religious feeling; but intensity is no substitute for quality. Compared with the early Muslim students of Greek philosophy, to whom they have sometimes
claimed a relationship, they are theologically null. And if,
as has been said, the quality of a nation's religion is reflected in that nation's culture, the confusion of principles
and the base alloy of thought which they have introduced
into Islamic religion bodes ill for the future of Muslim
culture, if its standards are to be set by them.

One notable voice has, however, been raised to rebuke
the superficiality of these modernist essays in revaluation
and to demand a fresh examination of the fundamentals of
Islamic belief. It is the voice of Sir Muhammad Iqbāl, in
those six lectures on the reconstruction of religious

thought in Islam which have already been mentioned in passing. Iqbāl makes no attempt to conceal the part played by Western thought in stimulating his attempt:

> The most remarkable phenomenon of modern history . . . . is the enormous rapidity with which the world of Islam is spiritually moving towards the West. There is nothing wrong in this movement, for European culture, on its intellectual side, is only a further development of some of the most important phases of the culture of Islam. . . . . No wonder, then, that the younger generation of Islam in Asia and Africa demand a fresh orientation of their faith. With the reawakening of Islam, therefore, it is necessary to examine, in an independent spirit, what Europe has thought, and how far the conclusions reached by her can help us in the revision and, if necessary, reconstruction, of theological thought in Islam [p. 7].

In a later passage the qualifying condition is dropped and the necessity of a new formulation of Islamic theology openly proclaimed:

> Nor can the concepts of theological systems, draped in the terminology of a practically dead metaphysics, be of any help to those who happen to possess a different intellectual background. The task before the modern Muslim is, therefore, immense. He has to rethink the whole system of Islam without completely breaking with the past. . . . . The only course open to us is to approach modern knowledge with a respectful but independent attitude and to appreciate the teachings of Islam in the light of that knowledge, even though we may be led to differ from those who have gone before us [p. 92].

In his pursuit of the new interpretation, Iqbāl leads the inquiring Muslim through very deep waters indeed. Beginning with an analysis of religious experience, he proceeds to examine its philosophical content and finds it in the concept of pure duration. Serial time, with its sequence of cause and effect, is simply the creation of the logical mind in attempting to grapple with the world of space. The universe is not "the temporal working-out of a preconceived plan" but "a free creative movement," ever expanding. The traditional concept of destiny was based on a materialist teleology which ignored "the progressive formation of fresh ends, purposes, and ideal scales of value as the process of life grows and expands" (pp. 51–52). Pure duration as an organic unity can be conceived only as the unity of a self, the Absolute or Ultimate Ego, eternally creative, to which nature (defined in Professor Whitehead's phrase as "a structure of events") stands in the same relation as character to the human self. Hence the observation of nature, that is to say, physical science, "is only another form of worship" (pp. 53–54).

In the third lecture Iqbāl develops his conception of the Ultimate Ego, to whom the Koran "in order to emphasize [His] individuality gives . . . . the proper name of Allah" (p. 59). Taking one by one the attributes of Creativeness, Knowledge, and Omnipotence, he expounds the atomic theory of the Muslim scholastics in the light of modern physics, the concept of Divine Knowledge as some indefinable relation "in the organic whole of God's creative life" (p. 75), and the Divine Omnipotence "as intimately related to Divine Wisdom" and "revealed, not in the arbitrary and the capricious, but in the recurrent, the regular, and the orderly" (p. 76).

This leads up to a discussion of the problem of evil. Iqbāl maintains insistently throughout his lectures that the Koran teaches the doctrine of the creative freedom of the human ego. In this connection he develops the koranic story of the Fall of Adam as a parable of "man's rise from a primitive state of instinctive appetite to the conscious possession of a free self, capable of doubt and disobedience" and "the emergence of a finite ego who has the power to choose." "That God has taken this risk shows his immense faith in man; it is for man now to justify this faith" (pp. 80–81). "But the acceptance of self-hood . . . . involves the acceptance of all the imperfections that flow from the finitude of self-hood" (p. 83).

The individuality and freedom of the human ego form the main subject of the next lecture. The real personality of the ego is not a thing, but an act, and its reality lies in its directive attitude (p. 98). "The body is accumulated action or habit of the soul" and matter "a colony of egos of a low order out of which emerges the ego of a higher order, when their association and interaction reach a certain degree of co-ordination" (p. 100).

With this, Iqbāl launches his challenge to the traditional orthodox theology:

> Nor is there such a thing as a purely physical level in the sense of possessing a materiality, elementally incapable of evolving the creative synthesis we call life and mind, and needing a transcendental Deity to impregnate it with the sentient and the mental. The Ultimate Ego that makes the emergent emerge is immanent in nature, and is described by the Quran as "the First and the Last, the visible and the invisible" [p. 101].

In contrast to this, the "morally degrading" doctrine of fatalism was invented by applying an inadequate philosophy of time to defend the opportunism of secular rulers and "support vested interests" (p. 105).

Finally, the koranic doctrine of immortality is partly ethical, partly biological. "It is open to man . . . . to belong to the meaning of the universe and become immortal" (p. 112). "Life offers a scope for ego-activity, and death is the first test of the synthetic activity of the ego." Death "is only a kind of passage to what the Quran describes as 'Barzakh' " or an intermediate stage of existence,[9] and "the records of Sufistic experience indicate that Barzakh is a state of consciousness characterized by a change in the ego's attitude towards time and space"—a state in which the ego "prepares himself for adjustment" to "fresh aspects of reality" (pp. 113–14).

> Heaven and Hell are states, not localities. Their descriptions in the Quran are visual representations of an inner fact, i.e., character. Hell, in the words of the Quran, is "God's kindled fire which mounts above the hearts"—the painful realization of one's failure as a man. Heaven is the joy of triumph over the forces of disintegration. There is no such thing as eternal damnation in Islam. . . . . Hell . . . . , as conceived by the

Quran, is not a pit of everlasting torture inflicted by a revengeful God; it is a corrective experience which may make a hardened ego once more sensitive to the living breeze of Divine Grace. Nor is Heaven a holiday. Life is one and continuous. . . . . Every act of a free ego creates a new situation, and thus offers further opportunities of creative unfolding [pp. 116–17].

This may, I hope, convey an adequate idea of the general direction of Iqbāl's philosophical thought. To the conservative Muslim it must seem a production of breathtaking audacity; and, though it has strongly influenced the younger intellectuals of India, I cannot think it has yet had any deep effect upon Muslim thought as a whole. Indeed, had it not been for Iqbāl's prestige as a poet and leader in Indian Islam, it is doubtful whether so revolutionary and heretical a work would ever have been published.

For us it is deeply interesting as an extreme illustration of certain basic tendencies in modernism. Note, in the first place, how closely it follows what an eminent theologian has recently described[10] as the fundamental presuppositions or prejudices of liberal theology, namely, that the essentials of religion are comprehended under (1) the nature and existence of God, (2) the moral freedom and responsibility of man, and (3) the immortality of the soul—all three in composition with scientific thought and the ideas of natural law and evolution. All unconsciously, Iqbāl was importing into Islam the same tendencies in thought as have in the West been gradually transforming Christianity into a religion of humanism.

In the second place, it cannot have escaped notice that this humanism of Iqbāl's finds its most congenial expression in the essentially antirational philosophy of Bergson. In his view all mystical experience and Sufi thought in Islam lead up to and find their interpretation in the doctrine of emergent evolution:

In his inmost being man, as conceived by the Quran, is a creative activity, an ascending spirit who . . . . rises from one state of being to another: ". . . . from state to state shall ye be surely carried onward" (Quran 84, 17–20). It is the lot of man to share in the deeper aspirations of the universe around him and to shape his own destiny as well as that of the universe, now by adjusting himself to its forces, now by putting the whole of his energy to mould its forces to his own ends and purposes. And in this process of progressive change God becomes a co-worker with him, provided man takes the initiative: "Verily God will not change the condition of men, till they change what is in themselves" (Quran 13, 12) [pp. 11–12].

In the third place, there is a complete dislocation between the argument and its supposed bases. What Iqbāl has done in these lectures is something quite different from what he set out to do. He aimed to reconstruct the established theology of Islam; but the theology which he attempts to restate is not, in fact, the orthodox theology but the Sufi theology. Where the other modernists have preached a new liberal and humanist Islam on the old orthodox foundations, Iqbāl has tried to refashion Sufi thought in terms of Western humanism. And this is not in any way controverted by the fact that in his lectures, as in his poetry, he over and over again criticizes Sufism and its pantheist tendencies.

The paradox in which Iqbāl was thus entangled is perhaps to be explained by the fact that what lies behind his thought is the Sufi theology, not the Sufi ethic. It was the Sufi ethic that Iqbāl hated, because to him it was the symbol and source of passivity and resignation. And it is just here that his chief weakness as a religious thinker lies, for Sufism, without its ethical and ascetic disciplines, runs to seed and becomes—as Iqbāl himself expressed it—"the pursuit of a nameless nothing." Nowhere in these lectures does he specify the moral imperatives of his system of thought. His concluding words are: "Let the Muslim of today appreciate his position, reconstruct his social life in the light of ultimate principles, and evolve, out of the hitherto partially revealed purpose of Islam, that spiritual democracy which is the ultimate aim of Islam." We shall see later on that he was not prepared to accept the concrete ethic of the Koran without qualification and reiterated his demand for a reinterpretation in harmony with his doctrine of the "dynamic outlook" of the Koran. And so we come back to his old gospel of dynamism, activism, and the Superman—a gospel whose moral imperatives we have learned to know too well to need any elaboration here.

The more one examines his argument, the more clearly one sees that Iqbāl shares a weakness which is common to all the modernists. Throughout the lectures he constantly appeals to koranic verses in support of his arguments. But we cannot help asking ourselves two questions: "Do these quotations represent the whole teaching of the Koran on the point at issue?" and "Do they mean what Iqbāl says they mean?" In one or two instances I suspect actual philological misinterpretations; but more generally there is an obvious strain between the plain sense and religious purport of the verse and the doctrine to which Iqbāl has fitted it. To discern a doctrine of serial and nonserial aspects of duration in texts relating to the alternation of the day and night and to creation in six days and in the twinkling of an eye (pp. 43 ff.) or the possibility of a new kind of individuality after death in "Now know We what the earth consumeth of them and with Us is a book in which account is kept" (p. 116) calls for a very vivid imagination. And in this, too, he exemplified another characteristic with which the critic previously cited has reproached liberal theology: "There was no way for Liberalism of carrying the business through which did not involve picking and choosing . . . . on a scale and with an arbitrariness quite impossible to justify, and then imposing interpretations on what was accepted which were very far indeed from the original intention of the words."[11]

We must surely give Iqbāl credit for courage and sincerity. But courage and sincerity are not enough. Nor can we even accept the plea that in his new theology he at least laid a foundation on which others might build after him, clarifying his vision and supplying an appropriate ethical content. As Dean Lowe has said: "However attractive it may be to find deeper, inner meanings in a limited number of passages . . . . the risk of arbitrariness and subjectivity offsets any possible gain. Once the path of mystical interpretation is entered, anything can mean anything."[12] Iqbāl's protest, in fact, fails on precisely the same grounds as the apologetic of the earlier modernists. On the basic issue of intellectual integrity, he did nothing to correct and much to confirm the cardinal error of all modernist thought—that while you may make your own religion what you choose, when you are dealing with the historic religious community, choosing is the sign of immaturity and of spiritual presumption.

CHAPTER V

LAW AND SOCIETY

FROM the modernist religious apologetic in the narrower sense, we turn now to the social attitudes of Muslim modernism. Since social ethics, social institutions, and law are, in principle, functions of the religious system in Islam, all these questions are tied up with religious orthodoxy to a much greater extent than they are in our Western civilization. The newer currents of thought on these subjects consequently flow in two different channels, which can be distinguished, theoretically at least, as the channel of reform and the channel of apologetic. But in practice it is sometimes difficult to say whether what appears to be apologetic is not really a disguised effort toward reform, by the device of defending what the writer asserts to be the genuine teaching of Islam on specific social questions.

Islam has often been described as a "totalitarian" religion. But all religious ideas that shape the imaginative outlook and content of the human mind and that determine the action of the human will are potentially or in principle totalitarian. They must seek to impose their own standards and rules on all social activities and institutions from elementary schools to law and government. Judaism is in this sense totalitarian; so also is Christianity. If we have forgotten it, it is only because from its earliest years Christianity was forced to recognize the authority of Roman law and because, when it seemed to be on the point of victory in its long struggle with Germanic feudalism in the Middle Ages, it had to suffer the assault of two new and deadly enemies: humanism and science. And science itself is coming very near to evolving a totalitarian idea, after breaking down the opposition of religion by its alliance with humanism and economic liberalism. If we may judge by the foretastes of it in Germany and Russia, indeed, scientific totalitarianism is preparing for the world a strait jacket of a stiffness and harshness beyond anything yet experienced by the human race.

Compared with this, the totalitarianism of a religious faith is a light and easy yoke. However "obscurantist" the religious authorities may be, they at least recognize the value and personality of the individual and so preserve for it a considerable range of liberty. In Islam, as we have seen, this liberty was further extended by the looseness of its organization, the absence of a hierarchy, and the principle of toleration of differences. But, like all totalitarian regimes, it attempted to control or to prevent the communication and spread of "dangerous thoughts."

It is worth our while to look a little more closely at the implications of this concept of "dangerous thoughts." Dangerous to what? To the fate of the individual? After all, if a man chooses to run the risk of eternal punishment in hell, that is his private affair. To purity of doctrine and the salvation of the community, which might be put in jeopardy by contamination? Possibly; but this is a little inconsistent in a society which recognizes "consensus" as normative. But discord in doctrine may lead to division and strife—this is the crux. The underlying conception is that a society cannot be stable unless it is permeated by the ethic deriving from a sound religious belief. The ethic cannot be stable unless the religious belief is maintained free from heterodox influences. Thus, not only is the preservation of the ethic more important than the flexibility and adaptability of society, it is the sole condition upon which the society can develop in the right direction, i.e., toward a higher degree of social integration and a more balanced life for the individual.

In other words, the kind of society that a community

builds for itself depends fundamentally upon its beliefs as to the nature and purpose of the universe and the place of the human soul within it. This is familiar enough doctrine and is reiterated from Christian pulpits week after week. But Islam is possibly the only religion which has constantly and consistently aimed to build up a society on this principle. The prime instrument of this purpose was law. "The science of Law," in the words of one of the famous Muslim definitions, "is the knowledge of the rights and duties whereby man is enabled to observe right conduct in this life, and to prepare himself for the world to come."

Unlike the law which Christendom inherited from Rome, therefore, Islamic law takes into its purview relationships of all kinds, both toward God and toward men, including such things as the performance of religious duties and the giving of alms, as well as domestic, civil, economic, and political institutions. By its origin, nature, and purpose it is intimately bound up with the religious ethic. It is true that ethical judgments are concerned less with the outward facts of a given action than with motives and ends and that a formulated legal system has generally to be satisfied with the external facts. But their spirit and ultimate bases are the same. Both rejected the utilitarian argument that certain actions are good because of their social consequences, even if it could be (and often was) demonstrated that, in fact, they did produce desirable social consequences. It followed that Islamic law was not regarded (like Roman or modern law) as the gradual deposit of the historical experience of a people. Its primary function was to classify actions in terms of an absolute standard of good and evil; the fixing of penalties for infractions of the standard was a quite secondary matter.

Now an absolutely valid standard of good and evil is not a thing which can be rationally determined. We have seen, in the first chapter, how the Muslim mentality rejected all those ideal general concepts from which absolute standards could theoretically be deduced. The only means by which they could be known was revelation, for God alone knows what is absolutely good or absolutely evil, and it is, indeed, only by His determination that they are so. Consequently, the legal system of Islam begins with the Koran, and it evolved side by side with, and on the same lines as, the theological system. The legal maxims found in the Koran or deduced from it were supplemented by the authoritative traditions of the Prophet and further supplemented and cemented by the infallible consensus of the community. The four "schools" of Hanafites, Malikites, Shaficites, and Hanbalites are legal, rather than doctrinal, schools; and the dissident theological sects also constructed and developed their own legal systems on parallel lines.

We need not go further here into the principles and methods of these legal systems. It is more relevant to our purpose to appreciate the interaction between Muslim law and Muslim society. Every legal system presupposes that those persons to whom it applies are willing to recognize its authority and acknowledge it as binding upon them, even though they may from time to time take the risk of contravening its specific injunctions. The acceptance of Islamic law, then, was conditional upon the acceptance of the religion of Islam, but it also followed inevitably from the fact of becoming Muslim. The religion of Islam was accepted by a large number of societies, each of which had a long social and legal tradition of its own. In adopting Islam as their religion, the members of those societies also accepted in principle the authority of Islamic law.

It is obvious, however, that old social and legal traditions and institutions could not simply be abolished at a stroke. The religious leaders of Islam have, in fact, had to engage in a long and arduous struggle to extend the actual jurisdiction of Islamic law among all these peoples.[1] In this struggle they gained a very considerable measure of success, though there are still groups, like the Berbers of

Northwest Africa, who are intensely Muslim in feeling but have even yet preserved their customary law in face of all the efforts of the ulema. Granted all this, however, the ulema, to the extent in which they have succeeded in imposing Islamic law, succeeded in unifying Islamic society, since the law, as I have suggested, was the instrument by which the social ethic of Islam was consolidated.

But here there are some distinctions to be drawn. Although the law embraced, in theory and in the exposition of the jurists, every branch and aspect of social relations, yet there were large areas in the life of the community where it was in practice ignored. The political and administrative institutions, a large part of penal jurisdiction, and most large-scale commerce lay outside its range of effective action, even if their procedures might sometimes be accommodated within its framework by means of legal fictions. Now it was precisely in these areas and among the classes concerned with them that European influences were first felt and have been most enduring and pervasive. This fact goes a long way to explain the—at first sight surprising—weakness of the resistance to the introduction into one Muslim country after another of constitutions, administrations, and penal, commercial, and civil codes based on European models, until today only Arabia and to some extent Afghanistan preserve the old Islamic legal institutions. It may even help to explain why the liberal modernists (since their ranks are largely recruited from those classes among whom the authority of the religious law was never absolute) so often take up a Western—that is to say, a critical and secular—attitude to questions of Islamic law.

But there was one domain, on the other hand, in which the social legislation of Islam was firmly intrenched—the domain of personal relations, including marriage, divorce, and inheritance. The reason for the firmness of its hold here lies not only in the universality of these relations, affecting, as they do, every member of the society, but still more in the fact that the basic regulations are clearly laid down in the Koran. As we have seen, no Muslims, except the very small rationalist groups, are yet prepared to question that the Koran is the very Word of God. To men who hold this belief the idea of changing or abrogating these fundamental laws is equivalent to apostasy. If, in any system, the gap between the conviction that change is necessary and the actual change in the law is not easily or quickly bridged, here (one would say) it can be effected only by a revolution, such as has taken place in Turkey. It is for this reason that in every Muslim country except Turkey the personal statute of Muslims continues to be administered not by the civil courts but by the religious or Sharᶜi courts. Not only so but, by the logical application of the same principle, the members of every different religious community have their own religious courts to administer their personal statute according to their respective systems of canon law.[2]

This field of personal relations, however, is precisely the one in which the modernist demand for reform and the controversy between modernists and conservatives are most vigorous. There can be no doubt that the social conscience of the educated classes is deeply stirred by the abuses associated with the practices of polygamy and divorce. To a lesser degree they are alive also to the serious consequences of the koranic law of inheritance and of the law (not directly based upon the Koran) which permits the constitution of inalienable family endowments. The Koran prescribes in minute detail the shares and proportions in which property is to be distributed among heirs and allots to female heirs, in general, half the shares of the equivalent male heirs. It is not difficult to make out a case for the equity of these rules when applied to movable property (which was the ordinary form of property in Arabia); but, when applied to agricultural lands or to industrial capital, the effects can be economically disastrous in given circumstances. As for inalienable family *waqfs*, or endowments (which were, in large measure, a device to overcome the koranic restrictions), they also have been the cause of much moral corruption and economic loss, and for some time past there has been a strong agitation in Egypt and some other countries to abolish the practice.[3]

It is easy to understand and to sympathize with the sincere Muslim reformer in the dilemma in which he may find himself. He is up against not merely the authority of a social tradition, which has more than a thousand years of unquestioned rule behind it, or the inertia of long-ingrained habit, or the natural reluctance of the average man to give up the privileges which he has enjoyed for so long. He has, above all, to face the fact that these social traditions and habits claim to be supported by direct and unambiguous texts in the Koran. For the secularist this obstacle does not have the same importance and validity, although secularists also, of course, are at pains to forestall the religious argument, so that one is not always sure whether a given book or article on the "women's question" in Islam is the work of a secularist or of a modernist reformer.

Examples of purely secularist argument can no doubt be found in recent Turkish literature and in India; more doubtful is the degree to which they represent any large body of Muslim opinion, except possibly in Turkey. For our present purposes it is more important to look at some of the ways in which Muslim reformers and apologists have tried to meet the difficulties.

In one of his most famous poems, which is quoted also by Iqbāl, the Turkish poet and sociologist, Ziya Gök Alp (d. 1924), appealed for recognition of the legal equality of women:

> There is the woman, my mother, my sister, my daughter;
> It is she who calls up the most sacred emotions from the
> depths of my being.

There is my beloved, my sun, my moon, and my star;
It is she who teaches me to understand the poetry of life.
How could the Holy Law regard these beautiful creations
    as contemptible?
Surely the learned have erred in the interpretation of
    the Koran?

The foundation of the nation and of the state is the family;
So long as the full worth of the woman is not realized,
    the life of the nation remains incomplete.
The upbringing of the family must correspond with justice;
Therefore equality is necessary in three things—in
    divorce, in separation, and in inheritance.
So long as the woman is counted half the man in inheritance
    and one quarter of the man in marriage,
Neither the family nor the country will be raised up.[4]

But Ziya Gök Alp did not remain content with poetical protests; as a sociologist he undertook to find the principles by which the law could be reinterpreted. For this purpose he distinguished between the "divine" elements and the "social" elements in the Sharīᶜa. The "social" elements, in his view, were based not on textual revelation but on ᶜurf. This word, which in the terminology of the jurists means "customary law," he defined as "the value-judgments of a people or of a given community." Consequently, personal or family law was open to modification in whatever way might be demanded by "collective opinion" (i.e., ijmāᶜ) or by "the national conscience." Obviously, however, this attempt to draw distinctions is purely subjective; and the setting of customary law on an equal footing with the revealed law, even if it is regarded as the deposit of the historical experience or the character of a given nation, is irreconcilable with the bases of Islamic thought.[5]

I do not know of any writings by Arabic modernists which adopt a similar line of argument. The earlier Arab representatives of the feminist movement pressed, on the whole, for the removal of social rather than of legal disabilities. The Iraqi poet, Jamīl Sidqi az-Zahāwi, for example, was one of the first and most fearless critics of the social subjection of women and called again and again for a nobler and truer attitude toward them:

> Woman and man are no other than equal in worth;
> Educate the woman, for the woman is the symbol of culture.[6]

Still more outspoken is his poem entitled "Unveil!":

Take off the veil! For the veil, O daughter of Fihr, is a malady that saps the life of society.

Everything moves on to renovation, then why should this antiquity remain unchanged?

No command for the veil in this form has been given by any Prophet, nor approval expressed by any sage.

Alike in the eyes of the Sacred Law and of Nature, and in taste and reason and conscience is it blameworthy. . . . .

They have claimed that in the veil there is protection; they lie, for it is in truth a disgrace.

They have claimed that unveiling is a breach of modesty; they lie, for unveiling is perfect purity.

It is not the veil which guards the virtue of the girl; her guard is her upbringing and sharing in knowledge.

Cultivate the minds of the maidens, so that thereby the bodies of the maidens may remain secure from evil.[7]

Az-Zahāwi, however, rarely does more than hint at the marriage and divorce laws. More outspokenly, a Tunisian socialist, Tāhir al-Haddād, published in 1930 a book on *Our Women in the Religious Law and in Society*, in which he maintained that the laws of the Koran and the constructions of the Muslim legists must be regarded not as final and unalterable but from an evolutionary standpoint. The spirit of Islamic culture, he argued, demands a continual process of adaptation of their specific prescriptions to the development of civilization.[8] The modern Arabic literature of Egypt also, in its portrayal and analysis of social problems, is penetrated by an implicit criticism of the legal obstacles to the full equality of women.

More striking still, among the first projects mooted by the new Ministry of Social Affairs set up in Egypt in 1939 was one to restrict polygamy and to limit the conditions of divorce. But, although the proposals put forward by the ministry amounted to no more than a very moderate instalment of the reforms desired by educated opinion, they called out an immediate remonstrance from representatives of the Azhar point of view that they were contrary to the Sharī'a and that the ministry would be more worthily employed in turning its attention to horse-racing, betting, and other social evils denounced by the Koran and by Muslim ethics.

The true modernist cannot escape from his dilemma by such an easy cutting of the knot. The Koran must be true and final. And yet he is uneasily conscious that there is something amiss in the current Muslim social ethic. At the same time, it deeply wounds his feelings as a Muslim and his self-respect as a man to find that the only thing which the average Westerner knows about Islam is that a Muslim may have four wives; and the cruder missionary exploitation of his difficulties rubs salt into his wounds. He can see one, and only one, way out. The divinely given ethic of Islam cannot fall short in any way of the highest standards. Consequently, the medieval jurists must have in some respect deviated from the true spirit of the Koran and of Islam.

These deviations must be tracked to their source and discredited. When they have been cleared away, the original teachings of the Koran and of the Prophet will reappear in all their purity, their loftiness, and their even-handed justice toward both men and women. These teachings will be concerned primarily with general attitudes; they will define the spirit in which the law is to be conceived and applied rather than the letter of the law itself. That spirit, in relation to women, cannot be other than one of human sympathy, of respect for their personality, and readiness to redress the wrongs inflicted upon them by the harsh and imperfect functioning of society. Only after this spirit is thoroughly appreciated and absorbed will the specific legislation of the Koran be properly understood. When all is done, the modernist claims, it will be seen that the Muslim attitude toward women, the Muslim conception of their personality and their social status, the Muslim legislation for their protection, are the highest and most humane of their kind, far surpassing those of any other religion.

This, then, is the task before the modernist. The primary function of the modernist apologetic, it must be repeated, is to restore faith in Islam among doubting Muslims by demonstrating the supreme excellence of their religion. Its second function is to persuade the "old-fashioned" Muslims that they, by their social conservatism and their stand upon the letter of the law, are sinning against the light. But side by side with this the modernist cannot resist the opportunity of wiping the smirk off the missionary's face by a violent denunciation of the sexual ethics of Christianity and a selection of relevant examples from the history and the social documentation of so-called Christendom. As in dealing with religious questions, therefore, apologetic and controversy are rarely separated. And it is not surprising that to Muslims who know the West only from the life of the great cities and from Western films, novels, and magazines, the sexual ethics and standards of Western society are beneath contempt.

Since it would obviously be impossible to deal with some hundreds of thousands of books and pamphlets and to sum up their contents, the general lines of modernist argument can scarcely be better illustrated than by analyzing the chapter devoted by Sayyid Amīr Ali to "The Status of Women in Islam."[9] It is true that the writer was a Shiʿite and that he adopts a rationalist standpoint toward the Koran. But he presents practically the whole range of modernist and apologetic argument on the subject, and more persuasively than most of the later writers and pamphleteers, who repeat his assertions in every Muslim language in more violent or more restrained tones.

In certain stages of social development, polygamy, or more properly speaking, polygyny,—the union of one man with several women,—is an unavoidable circumstance. The frequent tribal wars and the consequent decimation of the male population, combined with the absolute power possessed by the chiefs, originated the custom which, in our advanced times, is justly regarded as an unendurable evil.

The scientific tone, followed by the outspoken condemnation, in this first paragraph is impressive. It is followed by a series of brief notes on the marriage customs of various ancient races (selecting the most unfavorable features and based mainly on biased secondary works) and an argument that the early Christian church openly or tacitly permitted the practice of polygamy. "Even the clergy . . . . availed themselves of the custom of keeping several left-handed wives by a simple license obtained from the bishop or the head of their diocese."[10] "The greatest and most reprehensible mistake committed by Christian writers is to suppose that Mohammed either adopted or legalised polygamy." He found it practiced not only among the Arabs but also among the Persians and the Jews, together with many other customs degrading to women.

The Prophet of Islam enforced as one of the essential teachings of his creed, "respect for women." And his followers, in their love and reverence for his celebrated daughter, proclaimed her "the Lady of Paradise," as the representative of her sex. "Our Lady of Light" is the embodiment of all that is divine in womanhood,—of all that is pure and true and holy in her sex,—the noblest ideal of human conception. [It will be remembered that Amīr Ali was a Shiʿite.] And she has been followed by a long succession of women, who have consecrated their sex by their virtues. Who has not heard of the saintly Râbiʿa and a thousand others her equals?

The apologist goes on to claim, with a mixture of accuracy and exaggeration, that Muhammad secured to women rights which they had not previously possessed, that he "placed them on a footing of perfect equality with men in the exercise of all legal powers and functions," and that he restrained polygamy by limiting the "maximum number of contemporaneous marriages" to four, but with

the proviso that "if you cannot deal equitably and justly
with all, you *shall* marry only one." This proviso is regarded as extremely important; "as absolute justice in
matters of feeling is impossible, the Koranic prescription
amounted in reality to a prohibition."[11]

But polygamy depends on circumstances, and "the
elasticity of laws is the greatest test of their beneficence
and usefulness":

This is the merit of the Koranic provision. It is adapted alike for the
acceptance of the most cultured society and the requirements of the
least civilised. . . . . The blight that has fallen on the Moslem nations
is due to the patristic doctrine which has prohibited the exercise of independent judgment [*ijtihād*]. The day is not far distant when an appeal
to the Teacher's own words will settle the question whether the Mos-
lems will follow Mohammed or the Fathers of the Church, who have
misused the Master's name to satisfy their own whimsicalities, or the
capricious dictates of Caliphs and Sultans, whose obsequious servants
they were.[12] But such a consummation can only result from a general
progress in the conception of facts, and a proper understanding of the
Prophet's teachings. . . . . [As things are,] the feeling against polygamy
is becoming a strong social, if not a moral, conviction. It has become
customary among all classes of the [Indian Musulman] community to
insert in the marriage-deed a clause, by which the intending husband
formally renounces his supposed right to contract a second union during
the continuance of the first marriage. Among the Indian Musulmans
ninety-five men out of every hundred are at the present moment, either
by conviction or necessity, monogamists. . . . . It is earnestly to be
hoped that, before long, a general synod of Moslem doctors will authoritatively declare that polygamy, like slavery, is abhorrent to the
laws of Islam.

This discussion is followed by several pages devoted to
Muhammad's own marriages, to rebut the accusation that
they were due to self-indulgence and "conclusively establish that the man, poor and without resource himself, when
he undertook the burden of supporting the women whom
he married in strict accordance with the old patriarchal institution, was undergoing a self-sacrifice of no light a character." He then turns to the subject of divorce, which he
handles on lines similar to those of his argument on
polygamy.

This subject, he says, "has proved a fruitful source of misconception and controversy; but there can be no question that the Koranic laws regarding the treatment of women in divorce [*note:* not 'regarding divorce'] are of better humanity and regard for justice than those of any other scripture." Then come the usual scrappy notes about ancient usages and an argument that what Gibbon called "the ambiguous word which contains the precept of Jesus" was "laid down probably to suit the requirements of an embryonic community, and delivered verbally," though "it may be regarded as inculcating a noble sentiment."

Muhammad, though disapproving of divorce, found it "impossible, under the existing conditions of society, to abolish the custom entirely." "The custom was not an unmixed evil; and accordingly he allowed the exercise of the power of divorce to husbands under certain conditions." "The reforms of Mohammed marked a new departure in the history of Eastern legislation"; nevertheless, "the permission in the Koran has to be read with the light of the Lawgiver's own enunciations." "The Fathers of the [Islamic] Church," on the other hand, "have taken up the temporary permission as the positive rule, and ignored many of the principles of equity inculcated by the Master." But, for all that, "the rules laid down by the legists are far more humane and just towards women than those of the most perfect Roman law developed in the bosom of the [Christian] Church."

Lastly, the apologist attacks the problem of the seclusion of women, or *purdah*, as it is called in India. Beginning with the observation that it is one of the survivals of older institutions which "have had the tendency to retard the advancement of the Mohammedan nations," he allows that "the system of female seclusion undoubtedly possesses many advantages in the social well-being of unsettled and uncultured communities." Muhammad perceived its advantages, and it is possible that, in view of the wide-spread laxity of morals among all classes of people, he recommended to the women-folk the observance of privacy. But to suppose that he ever intended his recommendation should assume its present inelastic form, or that he ever allowed or enjoined the *seclusion* of women, is wholly opposed to the spirit of his reforms.

And he justly adds that "the Koran itself affords no warrant for holding that the seclusion of women is a part of the new gospel." Attention is drawn to the gloomy and bitter misogyny expressed by the Christian Fathers; the universal repression of women in Christianity at a time "when Mariolatry was recognised and practised by all classes"; and the immorality attested in the convents. "The rise of Protestantism made no difference in the social conditions or in the conception of lawyers regarding the status of women. Jesus had treated woman with humanity; his followers excluded her from justice." The source of that more exalted ideal of womanhood which has become current in the recent centuries is to be found in the chivalry of the desert, transmitted to the West by means of the Crusades and the troubadours. Even so, it was contaminated by the coarseness of "the barbarian hordes of Europe," whereas "in the early centuries of Islam . . . . women continued to occupy as exalted a position as in modern society." Moreover, in spite of the improvement in the social position of Western women, "what is their legal position even in the most advanced communities of Christendom?" Therefore,

the Teacher who, in an age when no country, no system, no community gave any right to woman, maiden or married, mother or wife, who . . . . secured to the sex rights which are only unwillingly and under pressure being conceded to them by the civilised nations in the twentieth century, deserves the gratitude of humanity. If Mohammed had done nothing more, his claim to be a benefactor of mankind would have been indisputable.

If this summary in any way misrepresents the character of Amīr Ali's argument, the misrepresentation is certainly not deliberate. It is, as will have been observed, the argument of defending counsel—here and there conceding an unimportant point in order to cover up tacit omissions, playing down his opponent's case, exaggerating (and even inventing) weaknesses in it, and equally exaggerating or inventing points in his own favor. Yet he makes his task much easier by his assumption throughout that the koranic legislation was the work of Muhammad himself and that "each age has its own standard." How much more, then, must those more orthodox apologists who are denied recourse to these supports rely upon the same casuistical and rhetorical devices in presenting the same case?

Yet there is no wilful deception in all this. It is the expression of a completely genuine belief combined with a strong feeling of resentment at the assumed superiority of the Christian social ethic. The superficiality of its historical method, the evasion of difficulties, the recourse to *ipse dixit*'s, are only the outcome of that intellectual confusion with which the whole modernist movement is burdened and which makes it easy to shut one's eyes to what one does not wish to see. Even Iqbāl is caught in the same snare.

In his sixth lecture, which deals with the problems of law and society, the unresolved conflict between the two currents of his thought is most clearly displayed. After referring to the "dynamic outlook of the Koran," which "cannot be inimical to the idea of evolution," he urges that "in a society like Islam the problem of the revision of old institutions becomes still more delicate, and the responsibility of the reformer assumes a far more serious aspect." "Islam, by means of its well-conceived institutions, has succeeded to a very great extent in creating something like a collective will and conscience" in the "heterogeneous mass" of its adherents.

In the evolution of such a society even the immutability of socially harmless rules relating to eating and drinking, purity or impurity, has a life-value of its own, inasmuch as it tends to give such society a specific inwardness, and further secures that external and internal uniformity which counteracts the forces of heterogeneity always latent in a society of a composite character. The critic of these institutions must therefore try to secure, before he undertakes to handle them, a clear insight into the ultimate significance of the social experiment embodied in Islam. He must look at their structure, not from the standpoint of social advantage or disadvantage to this or that country, but from the point of view of the larger purpose which is being gradually worked out in the life of mankind as a whole [pp. 158–59].

So far, this is not only sound Islamic doctrine but also (*pace* Mr. Smith) sound religious insight and a well-merited rebuke to the externality of the ordinary modernist approach to these questions. But Iqbāl goes on to say:

I know the Ulema of Islam claim finality for the popular schools of Mohammedan Law . . . . but since things have changed and the world of Islam is to-day confronted and affected by new forces set free by the extraordinary development of human thought in all its directions, I see no reason why this attitude should be maintained any longer. Did the founders of our schools ever claim finality for their reasonings and interpretations? Never. The claim of the present generation of Muslim liberals to reinterpret the foundational legal principles, in the light of their own experience and the altered conditions of modern life is, in my opinion, perfectly justified [pp. 159–60].

On turning to deal with our present subjects, however, he by-passes entirely the problem of divorce to concentrate on the easier problem of inheritance. Referring to the poem of Ziya Gök Alp which has been quoted above, he asks

whether the equality of man and woman demanded by him, equality, that is to say, in point of divorce, separation, and inheritance, is possible according to Mohammedan Law. I do not know whether the awakening of woman in Turkey has created demands which cannot be met . . . . without a fresh interpretation of foundational principles. . . . . In view of the intense conservatism of the Muslims of India, Indian judges cannot but stick to what are called standard works. The result is that while the peoples are moving the law remains stationary.

Unperturbed by this astonishing self-contradiction, he proceeds:

With regard to the Turkish poet's demand, I am afraid he does not seem to know much about the family law of Islam. Nor does he seem to understand the economic significance of the Quranic rule of inheritance. . . . . From the inequality of their legal shares it must not be supposed that the rule assumes the superiority of males over females. Such an assumption would be contrary to the spirit of Islam. The Quran says: "And for women are rights over men similar to those for men over women." The share of the daughter is determined not by any inferiority inherent in her, but in view of her economic opportunities, and the place she occupies in the social structure of which she is a part and parcel [pp. 160–61].

It will be granted, as I have already said, that a case can be made out for Iqbāl's view that "it is really by this apparent inequality of their legal shares that the law secures the equality demanded by the Turkish poet" (p. 162). But in attempting to prove that no assumption of the inferiority of females to males can be justified from the Koran, he has (quite unconsciously, I believe) shut his eyes to the fact that the immediately following words in the very verse which he has cited for this purpose are: "but men have a standing above women."[13]

If we turn from the theory of the modernists to their practice, we shall find some wide divergences. I am very doubtful whether, outside Turkey, there is to be found in the Islamic world today any considerable section of society in which women do enjoy something like the social equality which the modernists demand, except for the Westernized middle classes of Egypt. It is true that in many Muslim countries the education of women has made great strides and that there has been some general shift in the direction of the social emancipation of women; but even in Egypt their range of economic opportunity is still narrowly restricted. In India, as Mr. Smith has written, *purdah* "is still widely defended as the only alternative to the most horrible licence. . . . . Still to-day a very large number of otherwise intelligent, liberal and well-to-do Muslims observe *purdah*, or rather make their wives and daughters observe it. Thus the under-cover retreat from defence of polygamy to that of *purdah* almost stops at the latter outpost. . . . . The retreat stops virtually dead when it reaches segregation of the sexes."[14]

To this general rule, he asserts, Iqbāl was no exception:

He never understood, and he constantly fought against, those who deem that women too might share in the brave new world. He imagined European women heartless, hating maternity, love and life; he wanted to keep women "pure" and in subjection. For women he wanted no activism, no freedom, no vicegerency of God. . . . . Woman should remain as she has always been in Islam, confined, acquiescent to man, and achieving nothing in herself but only through others. She should remain a means to an end. Iqbal kept his own wives in *purdah*, and untiringly he preached to the world his conception of the ideal woman:

> The chaste Fatimah is the harvest of the field of submission,
> The chaste Fatimah is a perfect model for mothers. . . . .
> She who might command the spirits of heaven and hell
> Merged her own will in the will of her husband.
> Her upbringing was in courtesy and forbearance;
> And, murmuring the Quran, she ground corn.

And yet Iqbal towards the end must have recognized that he was wrong about women. There is a hint of this in his small poem ᶜ*awrat* . . . . [which] concludes:

> I too at the oppression of women am most sorrowful;
> But the problem is intricate, no solution do I find possible.[15]

Is it going too far to suggest that this confession of failure sums up the whole modernist position? The dilemma, real enough though it may seem to the Western-educated middle classes in Egypt and India, is no dilemma at all for the great body of Muslim society. It has arisen in these particular places and circles, not out of an organic evolution within Muslim society, but out of the superimposition of a different social order professing a social ethic which has never been accepted by any Eastern society as a universal rule, even though monogamy is, and always has been, the general social practice. The claim made by Iqbāl for "the present generation of Muslim liberals to reinterpret the foundational legal principles" is, in effect, a claim that a small, self-constituted minority shall remodel the social institutions of one-seventh of the human race. And what the moral and intellectual qualifications of that minority are for such a task we have already seen. No wonder that the religious leaders ask on what authority they propose to do this! They cannot claim, for all their ingenuity, the authority of the Koran or the authority of the prophetic tradition. There remains only one source of authority, that of *ijmā*ᶜ, the consensus of the community.

We need not doubt, I think, that the logic of history will, in the long run, as the modernists foresee, bring about widespread changes in the attitude of the Muslim community toward these problems. Already, indeed, the abuse of the liberty of divorce is recognized, in orthodox as well as in modernist circles, to be the cause of serious stresses in Muslim society;[16] and others are likely to arise as the education of women widens in range and quality.

It is to be put to the credit of the modernists that, in opposition to the secularists, who wish to sever social institutions from all connection with the religious ethic or law, they continue to recognize the essential relation between social behavior and religious belief. They have preserved enough of that Islamic solidarity in their thinking to see that, if society is to be reformed, reform must come through the religious channel and not independently of religion or even in opposition to it. Where they have erred is in assuming as the final objective an ideal determined by considerations external to their own society and in trying to force the two into relation with one another. This is to ignore the differences between Muslim society and the Western societies in composition, geographical and economic conditions, and intellectual outlook; and it can be achieved only at the cost of lifting the argument out of the plane of realities and evading the concrete issues.

It is safe to say that, when, eventually, such social

strains develop on a general scale within Islam by the forces of internal evolution, they will find their own appropriate solutions. These solutions will not necessarily coincide with our Western solutions but will be based on the proved experience and needs of the Muslim peoples. And we may be sure that the principles applied to their solution will be practical and realistic and far removed from the intellectual confusions and the paralyzing romanticism which cloud the minds of the modernists of today.

CHAPTER VI

ISLAM IN THE WORLD

A T THE end of the preceding chapter, I used the words "the intellectual confusions and the paralyzing romanticism which cloud the minds of the modernists of today." This was not merely, as it might have seemed, a kind of rhetorical flourish, rounding off an argument with a colorful phrase, not to be taken too seriously. The words were, indeed, carefully chosen in order to sum up in the briefest compass the two elements which, in both thought and action, have so far hindered the modernists from making a full and positive contribution to the progress of the Muslim community.

Looking back over the two preceding chapters, the reader will recall that, in the field of religious thought, the main influence of modernism was found to be directed to the substitution of the emotional cult of Muhammad for a rationally based and spiritually effective theology. So far has this gone in certain circles that Mr. Smith čan write—perhaps with a grain of exaggeration: "Muslims will allow attacks on Allah; there are atheists and atheistic publications and rationalist societies; but to disparage Muhammad will provoke from even the most liberal sections of the community a fanaticism of blazing violence."[1] However exalted a view we may take of the personality of the Prophet, this is not a progressive but a backward step—and that not on the score of the alleged fanaticism but because it involves the deflection of reason from its proper functions. Instead of being devoted to the task of restating in modern terms the Muslim interpretation of the universe, it has been made to serve the purpose of underpinning an emotional reaction to the challenge flung down to Muslim pride and self-respect in the name of Christianity.

Similarly, in the face of the problems of social ethics and institutions, we have seen a genuinely reformist impulse lamed by inherent intellectual contradictions and traversed by zeal to formulate an apologetic. It cannot be denied that the modernists are vividly conscious of the pressing need to do away with abuses which arise out of old custom, even though the more clear-sighted are aware also of the social dangers which wait upon changes too rapidly conceived and not supported by any large body of conviction or pressure of social circumstances. But their ineffectiveness to move Muslim opinion can be traced largely to two main causes: first, that they are unable to place the facts and arguments in clear and compelling perspective, because they have not yet formulated to themselves a coherent social ideal adapted to the needs of Muslims generally; and, second, that by their apologetic, which exaggerates, on the one hand, the social virtues of the Islamic system in the past and, on the other hand, the social evils prevalent in Western societies, they have strengthened the opposition of conservative opinion to their own case. The confusion of purposes resulting from the failure to think out their own position has been, in other words, further confounded by a strong infusion of historical romanticism in their thought.

When we turn now to examine the modernists' view of the historical past of the Islamic community and its place in the modern world, it would be strange if we did not find it still more strongly colored by romanticism. On religious matters it is necessarily circumscribed and controlled to a certain extent by the Koran and its basic theology. In their social programs the modernists cannot wholly shut their eyes to the actual facts and conditions of modern life. But in their historical outlook there is no external control to restrain the exuberance of the romantic

imagination, neither religion nor inherited tradition nor
enlightened public opinion. When Amīr Ali exclaims:
"Who has not heard of the saintly Râbiᶜa and a thousand
others her equals?" I wonder how many Muslim readers
have asked themselves to name even five of those "thousand others."

It is necessary at this point to define more precisely
what is implied in "romanticism." I need scarcely recall
here that the Romantic movement began in Europe as a
revolt against that complex of formal rules or canons of
taste and style which governed English and French literature in the eighteenth century. Basically, it was a demand
for the release of the imagination from the strait jacket of
imposed standards, a reaction against classicism in all its
forms and expressions, an idealization of the facts and
experiences of life and of nature. But its effects went much
deeper. By exalting the imagination against reason it
opened the way to the rejection of objective standards in
all fields of thought, and in conjunction with the belief in
evolution it led to a rejection of all ultimates.

In the Western countries where the Romantic revival
started, this subjectivism was simultaneously offset by
two other developments in nineteenth-century thought:
scientific determinism and the growth of historical method.
But it has not, I think, been sufficiently appreciated that
the expansion of Western civilization into eastern Europe
and Asia took place during the age of the Romantic revival. It not only coincided, therefore, with the rise of
nationalism but was intimately linked with it. Since romanticism is at bottom a popular revolt against imposed
order, it is related to the same category of ideas as that out-
burst of popular self-consciousness which lies at the roots
of nationalism. And, where the countervailing currents of
scientific and historical thought were either absent or too
weak to exercise any influence, it is not to be wondered at
that the two new forces—the political and the imaginative

—combined to produce the nationalist impulses and mythologies with which we are all familiar.

We must, however, be very clear in our minds that the thought-forces now operating in the Muslim world are forces which have been generated within the Muslim community, even though their emergence has been due very largely to the impact of the West or though the trend of their development has been partly determined by Western influences. This may seem self-evident, but it needs to be stressed. The outward effects of the world-wide extension of Western technology and skills are so patent to the most superficial observer that it is easy to slip into assumptions of a parallel extension of Western thought.

But these assumptions are quite unjustified, even if the Muslim modernist, on his side, believes in and asserts the identity of modern Muslim thinking with Western thinking. The inner effects of the impact of Western ideas are largely unconscious, and what is moving in the depths can rarely be more than guessed at. (I am not now referring, of course, to technical scientific production but to the processes of thought on religious, social, and historical questions.) All the same, our examination of the religious and social apologetic of modernism forces us to the conclusion that, out of the wide range of Western thought, only certain tendencies have found a response in Muslim minds, to the exclusion of other tendencies that might have been expected to exert some influence also.

How is this limitation to be accounted for? One explanation may be put forward here, even if only very tentatively. It will be recalled that in the first chapter I discussed the atomism, the discreteness, and the intensity of the Arab imagination, its resistance to synthetic constructions and, above all, its aversion from rationalism. We saw that only the orthodox religious institution had been able to establish some control over this tendency of the Arab

imagination to run wild, although even here the innate
tendency toward intuitive reason produced, alongside the
orthodox theology, a distinct type of mystical religion.

Western civilization, when it invaded the Muslim East,
was a web woven of many strands—so many, indeed, that
we should ourselves find some difficulty in disentangling
and identifying them all. Now it seems to be a general
rule of history that, when two civilizations come into
contact and a transmission of ideas is effected, the re-
cipients are attracted to those elements in the other civilization which are most congenial to their own habits of
thought and, on the whole, neglect or reject the other
elements which they find more difficult to assimilate. The
resemblance between the intuitive bent of the Arab and
Muslim mind and the Romantic currents in European
thought is certainly a very close one, and this may (I believe) explain the rapidity with which the Romantic
tendencies in Western thought spread among the educated
classes in Islam.

Iqbāl spoke more truly than he intended when he implied
that Muslims were only taking back from Europe "a
further development of some of the most important phases
of the culture of Islam." He was thinking of physical and
psychological theory; but what the Muslim intellectuals
did take back from Europe was, above all, the imaginative
legacy of romanticism, which had indeed been stimulated
in Europe by the influence of Arabic literature in the
Middle Ages and again by the popularity of the *Arabian
Nights* in the eighteenth century. The unconscious irony of
Iqbāl's claim is rendered still more striking by the fact
that he is himself the most conspicuous example of this
process, since the ideas expressed in his lectures on religious reconstruction are (as we have seen) the product of
the intuitive reasoning of the Sufi attracted into the orbit
of the high priest and prophet of Romantic antirational-
ism, Henri Bergson.

A further proof of the extent to which the new romantic movements in the Muslim world reflect a Western ideology is to be found in the direction taken in their development. Just as in Europe romanticism gave color and emotional appeal to a new nationalism founded on language, racial theory, and a historic past, so, too, the modernist apologetic and reform movement in Islam is combined with a nationalist interpretation of Islam, going back to Jamāl ad-Dīn al-Afghāni.

But there is one objection which may plausibly be urged against this view. Does not Islam postulate the unity of church and state? Is not the Khalīfa, the caliph, at the same time the religious head and the political chief of the Muslim community? Wherein, then, lies the novelty of the "nationalist interpretation"? Granted that it is not always easy to distinguish on the surface, nevertheless there is a deep spiritual cleavage between Islamic universalism and modern Pan-Islamism.

Although Islamic theory recognized the unity of church and state under the rule of the caliphate, that recognition assumed and was dependent on the function of the caliph as the instrument and representative of the sacred law. When the political systems in the Muslim world diverged from the theocratic ideal, the loyalty of Muslims to the political head was no longer absolute. Their first loyalty was to the ideals and institutions of Islam, and this might involve a negative attitude, or even demand a hostile attitude, to the secular rulers. This was, and is, the driving force behind the ideals of Mahdism and those manifestations of revolt against Ottoman rule which we studied in the second chapter.

Pan-Islamism, on the other hand, preached the doctrine of loyalty to the Ottoman caliph primarily as the head of the most powerful Muslim state, and therefore the authority most fitted to direct and to co-ordinate the political forces of the Muslim peoples. Pan-Islamic propaganda no doubt stressed the religious significance of the caliphate; but it was founded on an inner contradiction, which became more and more glaring as the policy of the Ottoman so-called "caliphate" moved further away from the principles of Islamic theocracy toward a pure secularism. Consequently, when the hour of testing came, during the first World War, Pan-Islamism proved itself a broken reed.

The disappearance of the Ottoman caliphate left the way open to three alternatives. The pure modernists toyed with the idea of creating a new kind of caliphate, of transforming it into a sort of spiritual directory which would be recognized by all Muslims as the authoritative exponent of the Faith and which, they perhaps overconfidently believed, would gradually reform the institutions of Islam in the spirit of their own programs. The origins of this idea may be traced to one or two Arab reformers at the beginning of this century,[2] but it found most favor in India and was expressly taken up by Iqbāl:

> The transfer of the power of Ijtihad from individual representatives of schools to a Muslim legislative assembly which, in view of the growth of opposing sects, is the only possible form Ijma can take in modern times, will secure contributions to legal discussion from laymen who happen to possess a keen insight into affairs. In this way alone we can stir into activity the dormant spirit of life in our legal system, and give it an evolutionary outlook [p. 165].

The secularists and the more nationalist Muslims, on the other hand, accepted the dissolution of the caliphate as final and devoted their energies to the building-up of national units, separate Muslim nations, whether monarchies or republics, on modern Western lines. It is outside the range of our present subject to discuss at length the political development of the modern nationalist movements. It is enough to say that a broad distinction can be drawn between two competing tendencies. One tendency, expressed in Arab nationalism and the Indian Muslim League, aims at uniting all the regions in which there is a community of language, race, or history into large Muslim states. The other is local or geographical nationalism, aiming at the erection of each region, such as Egypt or Iraq, into a separate political state and strengthening the regional self-consciousness of its inhabitants. I have called these "competing" tendencies; but, in fact, there are numerous cross-divisions which blur the frontiers between them, as well as the complications introduced by religious and sectarian differences, especially in India.

The third alternative is the revival of Mahdism, the assertion that the Muslim world must be purified and re-united by the sword. In contrast to the modernists and the nationalists, who represent differing applications of West-ern concepts to the political problems of Islam, this is a popular movement, reflecting the native impulses of the Arab and Muslim mind. It is the true product of primitive Islamic romanticism, with an emotional reason of its own. It is not a rational assertion that one type of political organization is more desirable than another, but a revolt against what is felt to be, in some particular relation, an intolerable state of affairs. In conformity with the atom-istic and discrete character of Arab and Muslim thought, the imagination and the effort are concentrated upon an immediate objective—the removal of something that can no longer be borne. What is to follow is left to the future to decide.

It is difficult to imagine that any of these alternatives holds out much hope for the future of Islam and of the Muslim community. All are vitiated by the emotional impulses characteristic of the Romantic outlook, with its disregard of historical thinking and its failure to grasp the fact that no endeavor can succeed unless it achieves a balance between the broad and deep currents of a people's psychology and the inescapable forces of social evolution.

The idea of a Muslim legislative assembly or spiritual directory rests upon the conception of a "spiritual Caliph-ate," divorced from temporal power and sovereignty.

However reasonable the phrase may sound in Western ears, it is doubly offensive to orthodox Muslim sentiment. In the first place, the caliphate is not a spiritual office; it exists solely as the instrument of the religious law, the Sharī‘a, which its holder is bound to carry out and which he has no power to modify or even to promulgate. Muslims owe spiritual allegiance to no person but to the law alone. So clearly and uniformly is this doctrine laid down that it seems more than a little strange that Muslim modernists should have deviated into the common Western error that the caliphate is a kind of papacy or can be resolved into a sort of ecumenical council. In the second place, if it is to enforce the Sharī‘a, the caliphate cannot be divorced from temporal sovereignty. All military and police forces must be under the caliph's control; otherwise his authority exists only on sufferance. All this is so self-evident that one hardly needs the explicit pronouncement of the editor of *Nūr al-Islām*, the official organ of the ulema of al-Azhar, that "one of the gravest of the innovations" put forward by the modernists is "a 'spiritual' Caliph without army or weapons" and that it is simply "a symbol for the separation of the Faith from political government."[3]

But there is more to it even than this. We saw in the first chapter that the Muslim conception of *ijmā‘* rests upon the religious conscience of the people as a whole. The spiritual democracy of Islam is total. It cannot tolerate a hierarchy, and without a hierarchy there can be no council with power "to loose and bind." Who would select the members? What powers would they have? And if, as the reformers desire, they were to controvert some of the decisions of the existing schools, what authority would their findings enjoy? Orthodox Muslim thought recognizes the principle of election in temporal matters—such as the choosing of a caliph—but the idea of elected or representative bodies in spiritual matters is totally foreign to it and borrowed from the West. The ulema may lead or direct, they cannot control, the conscience of the individual;[4] nor is there any guaranty that any body of ulema or any representative assembly will, in fact, interpret the conscience of the community as a whole. The instance I have already cited of coffee-drinking is a complete answer to any presumption of the sort.

In short, a council of this kind, so far from constituting a unifying force, would be only a factor of disunity and conflict within the Muslim community. In a society so broadly based, so cohesive in its texture, the sole instrument of adaptation to new conditions and new currents of thought must be the general will; and a general will, as we have already seen, can be built up only by gradual stages over a period of many generations. The basic heresy of the Muslim reformers is that ultimately they have no trust in the mass of men—in contrast not only to the Muslim tradition but also to the Protestant reformers—but seek to drive them toward a predetermined objective.

The nationalist solution is even more clearly opposed to the Islamic principle. No matter how sincerely nationalists may profess their devotion to the doctrines and the ethical teachings of Islam, they are committed to setting up a second principle alongside it; and there is no way to avoid the resulting division and conflict of duties except by separating the spheres of church and state. Muslim nationalists may plead that they hold the second principle to be subordinate to the first; but experience—even in Muslim countries—has shown that the appetite of the modern national state is not easily satisfied short of the total allegiance of its population. And the conflict of aims is fundamental: Islam, like all higher religions, seeks the interests and welfare of individual men and women irrespective of race and nation, while nationalism, of necessity, sacrifices the individual to the supposed interests of the collectivity.

If this be so, it may seem strange that the ulema should not have been outspoken in their condemnation of nationalism and should even appear to accept it as a legitimate political aspiration. Two considerations may perhaps help to explain their attitude. One is the failure to appreciate the real character of nationalism. They have, of course, observed its consequences in the outer world; but to observe consequences is by no means the same thing as to analyze their true causes; and it must be remembered that few of the ulema have access to the literature of political thought produced in Europe and America. In addition to this, they may reassure themselves by the belief that nationalism in the Muslim lands is quite different from nationalism in Europe and that it will never go to the same lengths but always remain on good terms with the Faith.

The second explanation lies in history. Part of the story lies in the atomism of the Muslim mind which, by its rejection of abstract "law," hindered Muslim thinkers from evolving a systematic and practical political doctrine. Islamic ethics, as we saw in the first chapter, furnished Muslims with a social ideal; the realization of this ideal seemed to offer them a practical objective of political thought. Since government could be truly directed toward human welfare only when it rested on and administered the sacred law, it must be essentially theocratic, with the political responsibility of the individual reduced to the reform of abuses. The learned, therefore, elaborated an ideal structure, a theory of a caliphate, which was in part deduced by purely logical processes from these premises, in part based on a romantic retrospect of the primitive caliphate (which had, in point of historical fact, irretrievably broken down in less than twenty-five years). Beyond this point orthodox thought rarely ventured into political economy or philosophy. After its ideal had been set up, nothing else mattered. With that refusal to admit of anything less than the ideal which is characteristic of the uncompromising perfectionist, Muslim thinkers regarded any kind of autonomous political institutions, independent of the sacred law in which the social ideal was enshrined, as either self-assertions of the uncontrolled animal appetite or the fanciful productions of rationalist thought.

The Muslim utopia suffered the usual fate of its kind. From the earliest centuries of Islam, political control was, in fact, exercised by secular governments. In the eyes of the ulema, they were no more than organizations of force for defense against external enemies and the maintenance of internal order, directed by self-constituted bodies of privileged persons and kept up by more or less illegal forms of taxation.

Toward such governments there were only two alternatives before the individual Muslim. One was to submit, on the principle that tyranny was preferable to anarchy; the other to assert by violence the supremacy of the sacred law. The ulema, with the general body of the community, have pretty consistently chosen the first alternative. So long as the secular governments did not interfere with the social institutions of Islam and formally recognized the Shariᶜa, the conscience of believers was not outraged and the task of building up a stable and universal Muslim society could go on. But long centuries of submission to secular government induced a tradition of political quietism which cannot easily or quickly be shaken off and still further inhibited the development of political thought and its application to changing circumstances. The rise of nationalism has thus taken the ulema unaware and found them unprepared to examine its religious implications.

The alternative attitude toward secular government—a violent assertion of the supremacy of the sacred law—is, as we have seen, the kernel of revolutionary Mahdism, which encourages and is itself sustained by the hope of a catastrophic reversal of the existing order and its replacement by the theocratic ideal. In its basic objective it coincides with the political theory of the orthodox ulema in that it limits the function of political government to securing the temporal framework for the unhindered operation of the sacred law and exercise of the Islamic ethic. This conception is, as I have tried to indicate, fundamental in Islam, and Mahdism is by no means an unmixed evil. There are times—and Islamic history is full of examples of them—when resort to violence is the only way open to men to overthrow an accumulation of evils and abuses and to make a fresh start.

But it is a solution of which the ulema are traditionally loath to approve, for many reasons. It is seldom that one can be sure that the leader of such a revolt is genuinely aiming to restore the supremacy of the Sharīʿa and capable of doing it, however enthusiastic his popular following. And, once violence is let loose, there is no saying where it may end. Long before the French Revolution, the ulema knew that revolution has a way of devouring its own children. Most Mahdist movements have generated a fierce sectarianism, which did not spare other Muslims.

It was thus not timidity, but prudence, which counseled restraint—that same prudence which is shown in the lawbooks by the proviso that the Jihād, the Holy War, may not lawfully be undertaken unless there is a reasonable prospect of its success. Over and above all this, the ulema had a profound sense of historical continuity and of their own responsibility for safeguarding it. This was, indeed, their primary and all-important function, expressed in the saying attributed to Muhammad: "The ulema are the heirs of the Prophet"; and a fleeting wave of enthusiasm was no substitute for the steady preservation of the social structure and the traditions of the community.

The further question which the Western observer is inclined to ask, namely, "How can a Mahdist movement secure the technical and economic progress which is essential if the Muslim peoples are to take their place on an equal footing with other peoples in a unitary world?" may not, perhaps, appeal with so much force to the ulema as to the modernists. But there is another element in modern Mahdism which has gone far toward transforming and obscuring its original character and purpose. Although Mahdism is the true product of primitive Islamic romanticism, it is no longer the pure and uncorrupted expression of that principle. Ever since the days of Jamāl ad-Dīn al-Afghāni, the leaven of nationalism has been working within it too.

To begin with, it was the other way round. There was an element of Mahdism in the Pan-Islamic nationalism of al-Afghāni, the element in his campaign that appealed to the popular masses and won for him the affection that has clung to his name. Although Muhammad Abduh rejected for himself this revolutionary taint, he did not exorcise it. It has survived in the modern reformist movement as a kind of ground swell, determining the ultimate nature of its thought and reactions, however much the surface features may seem to be in contradiction with it and however little the majority of modernists may be conscious of it. And it is this, probably, which explains the otherwise puzzling fact that so many modernists, finding the strain of double-mindedness too severe to be borne or the social cost of modernism to the individual too high, end up as ultra-orthodox bigots.

We must, however, make our lines of distinction as sharp as possible. Nationalism in its Western manifestations is confined to the intellectuals who are in direct and close touch with Western thought. As the nationalist idea penetrated into the popular mind, it was transformed, and could not avoid being transformed, by the pressure of the age-long instincts and impulses of the Muslim masses. For the vaguer ideals of Pan-Islam were substituted the concrete aspirations of Pan-Arabism and the parallel movements in India and Java, made more concrete still by the existence of definite local grievances and objectives and by the visible presence of the forces against which they were arrayed. Thus Mahdism has linked up with extreme nationalism to produce the swelling tides of popular discontent and revolutionary ardor which are familiar to all observers of the Muslim world today.[5]

If this analysis is not mistaken, the conclusion which seems to emerge is that the religious heritage of Islam is threatened not so much from without as by three forces from within. The first aims at substituting a social and this-worldly outlook and a utilitarian ethic for the stern discipline of a transcendentalist faith. The modernists are, in effect, repeating the error of the old Muᶜtazilites, by interpreting God in terms of their own minds. It is difficult to believe that the ultimate consequences of that endeavor would be very different in the Islamic world from what they have been in the Christian world. Even if we discount the argument from experience and the signs of movement in the same direction, it is self-evident that an Islam in which the humanizing elements were not balanced by an uncompromising transcendentalism would be a religion totally different from Islam as it was and is.

The second sets up the false gods borrowed from the West alongside Allah and attempts or claims to serve them all. This is *shirk*, "pluralism," the unforgivable sin. "Verily, Allah will not forgive the association of other gods with Him. Anything other than this He may forgive to whom He will, but whosoever associates other gods with Allah has conceived in his mind a falsehood of surpassing wickedness" (Koran 4:51). Even in its mildest and theologically least obnoxious forms, it involves the introduction of modes of thought and institutions alien to the social experience which is at the base of Islamic universalism and creates a confusion of ideals, which must inevitably have repercussions on the whole religious system, for I need only recall here the close and intimate connection between social structure and religious beliefs which, as we saw in the preceding chapter, Islam has always insisted upon as fundamental.

The third would throw away all those hard-won positions by which Islam consolidated its claims in the intellectual life of mankind and from which it must start in the new effort to establish their validity in the modern world. The heresy of Mahdism is its belief not only that the minds and wills of men can be dominated by force but that truth can be demonstrated by the edge of the sword.

Of these three forces, the third is probably the most dangerous. The religious intuition inherited by the Muslim peoples, the awareness of the unseen which Dr. Macdonald so strongly emphasized in his Haskell Lectures, all that solid core of religious feeling which finds satisfaction in Islam, are not likely to be seriously affected by modernist or secularist thought. Liberalism itself, as is proved by the superficiality of its effects, has struck no profound roots in the Muslim mind. Its principal result so far has been only to create a new division or schism, that between the Westernized intellectuals and the rest of the educated Muslims.

But what is going to happen when the technological processes of Western civilization penetrate more deeply into Muslim society, with more and more disturbing effects? Outwardly, the alternatives would seem to lie between an increasing secularism or a more violent Mahdist reaction—the choice depending in part upon the relations which develop between the Muslim peoples and the Western countries. But, given time and a world at peace, the result may just as well be a gradual reassimilation of the intellectuals, a closing-up of the split created by modernism in the forces opposed to both secularism and Mahdism, a reassertion of the cultural values for which Islam has traditionally stood, and the development of antitoxins to counteract the virus introduced from the West.

If this is to be realized, however, the Muslim faith will have to show that it possesses the strength and vitality to generate these antitoxins, mainly out of its own resources, but not excluding the possibility of adapting some of the constructive elements in Western thought in place of its destructive romanticism. The future of Islam rests where it has rested in the past—on the insight of the orthodox leaders and their capacity to resolve the new tensions as they arise by a positive doctrine which will face and master the forces making for disintegration.

One of the points on which modernist and Mahdist agree is in attacking the attitude of the ulema and their followers as "reactionary" or "conservative." To ardent reformers and revolutionaries it is never a welcome argument that old or traditional institutions express, as a rule, permanent tendencies in social life and relations and that violent changes produce much loss and little, if any, gain to the community as a whole. And their impatience is not lessened by the countercriticism of the ulema that the arguments which they put forward are based on ignorance and false judgment.[6]

At the same time, even if we discount the partisan criticisms of opponents, it seems impossible to deny that in the attitude and outlook of the ulema and their followers there is a disturbing weakness. They are losing touch with the thought of the age. Their arguments, however just, fail to carry conviction because they are expressed in thought-forms which arouse no response in the minds of educated men. Even the very language which they generally use has an antiquarian flavor that strikes curiously upon the ear and eye and strengthens the feeling that they have no message for today. Above all, their public pronouncements display a rigid formalism and reliance upon authority which, as the modernists see truly, are but feeble weapons of defense in the struggle with the forces arrayed against religion throughout the world.

These facts lend color to the accusations of those critics, both Western and Eastern, who describe orthodox Islam as a petrified religion. But the accusation is false. Islam is a living and vital religion, appealing to the hearts, minds, and consciences of tens and hundreds of millions, setting them a standard by which to live honest, sober, and god-fearing lives. It is not Islam that is petrified, but its orthodox formulations, its systematic theology, its social apologetic. It is here that the dislocation lies, that the dissatisfaction is felt among a large proportion of its most educated and intelligent adherents and that the danger for its future is most evident. No religion can ultimately resist disintegration if there is a perpetual gulf between its demands upon the will and its appeal to the intellect of its followers. That for the vast majority of Muslims the problem of dislocation has not yet arisen justifies the ulema in refusing to be rushed into the hasty measures which the modernists prescribe; but the spread of modernism is a warning that re-formulation cannot be indefinitely shelved.

In trying to determine the origins and causes of this petrifaction of the formulas of Islam, we may possibly also find a clue to the answer to the question which the modernists are asking, but have so far failed to solve— the question, that is, of the way in which the fundamental principles of Islam may be re-formulated without affecting their essential elements.

In briefest outline the source of the later difficulties can be traced back to the turning-point in the development of Islamic theology in the third and fourth centuries after the Hijra. In the second chapter I stressed, as we and Muslim scholars themselves are both, perhaps, too apt to do, its negative aspects—the rejection of the speculative universals of Greek thought. But there was also a positive side, without which, indeed, a systematic theology of Islam could not have been formulated, for theology is in its own field a scientific discipline and calls for the use of scientific tools. These tools, and more particularly deductive logic and physics, were taken over by the Muslim theologians and applied to their own postulates. Having done so, they could go no further along that line. Every scientific argument must always take the same course and always reach the same conclusion, unless you change the postulates or invent new tools, such as inductive for deductive logic.

The point of importance for us is that in and through theology Islam came to terms with scientific methods and modes of thought. This was a first and essential step. It delivered Islamic thought from the dangers inherent in the Romantic, that is the purely intuitive or imaginative, approach to the problems of existence and the universe. But there the development of orthodox thinking stopped, and there the process of petrifaction set in. Yet the solvent lay within the grasp of Muslim thinkers, if only they had perceived its significance and had come to terms with it as well. That solvent was the historical method and mode of thought.

That they failed to take this second step was not because the medieval Muslims had no conception of the problem of historical method. Almost from the first, the Arabic chroniclers had applied some principles of criticism to their materials, principles derived, in the first instance, from the methods of criticism evolved by the theologians themselves for the study of the prophetic tradition. This element of intellectual discipline, of historical rationalism, had made noteworthy progress by the third and fourth centuries. But, in proportion as it emancipated itself from theological control, it roused the suspicions and even the hostility of the theologians. Moreover, the historians never succeeded in overcoming the irrational and imaginative elements which were inherent in the character of their sources and materials or the theological influences deriving from the religious sciences. When, therefore, the intellectual decline set in, they accepted almost without protest the dogmatic reconstruction of the Islamic past which had gradually taken shape in orthodox circles and consented to serve the ends assigned to history by the ulema—those of an instrument of moral instruction and of dogmatic controversy.

Not only was this subordination of historical method and thought to the demands of religious emotion and theological dogma a sign of failure to move forward; but it was a reaction, a throwback to that play of the imagination which we have already seen in the early development of Islamic dogma. The later orthodox presentation of early Islamic history displays all the characteristics of prescientific historiography—its dramatic structure; the absoluteness of its judgments upon men and events; the capricious selection of materials; and, in addition, one feature which is not prescientific but betrays the propagandist, the exclusion of all detail that is in any way inconsistent with the picture which it is desired to convey. And, finally, this presentation was, like the dogmas of orthodox theology, invested with religious sanctions, so that to question it came to be regarded as heresy.

In thus forcing history to serve as a buttress of orthodox doctrine, the ulema barred the door to the last principle which could have preserved an element of flexibility in Islamic thought and prevented the petrifaction of its formulas. It is a curious blindness in the pietist imagination that, while it professes to regard history as the external manifestation of the Will of God in human society, it is never able to distinguish fact from the creations of its own imagining. It cannot perceive that, if God is in history, then to refuse to pursue the investigation of historical fact with an inexorable devotion to truth—and, worse still, to tamper with historical fact in order to force it into the framework of a preconceived scheme—is neither more nor less than a refusal to seek to learn the real purport of that manifestation of God's Will.

This reflection may seem a little hard upon the Muslim divines when we remember the very similar attitude adopted by our own medieval clergy and by no means discarded even yet by Christian pietists of all denominations. But when so many Muslim apologists declare that the spirit of Islam encouraged the fearless pursuit of truth in all its branches, it is fair to ask where the responsibility lies for the stifling of the spirit of historical inquiry in the later centuries of Islam. They have every right to point with pride to Ibn Khaldūn, that outstanding genius who attempted in the fourteenth century to construct afresh a scientific foundation for history. But his is precisely the case that confirms the argument; for, apart altogether from the fact than Ibn Khaldūn himself accepted most of the dogmatic affirmations of the orthodox view of history, his genuinely scientific and creative approach to the problem of historical method aroused not the faintest response in orthodox circles and remained neglected or forgotten until the resurrection of his work in the nineteenth century.

The practical outcome of this argument is that the way to the reconciliation of Islamic orthodoxy with the modern movement of thought lies not, as is so often supposed, through compromise with the hypotheses of modern science. The scientific habit of thought has never been lost by Muslim scholars, though they may very likely need to revise their scientific method and to broaden out as well as deepen their grasp of it. The way is to be found rather in revaluation of the data of thought through the cultivation of historical thinking. Only historical thinking can restore the flexibility demanded by this task, in proportion to its success in freeing the vision of the great overriding movement of the Eternal Reason from the frailties, the halting interpretations, and the fussy embroideries of its human instruments and agents. Only historical thinking teaches man the true measure of his stature and the humility that curbs theological and scientific arrogance. It is not an easy process, or always an agreeable one. Experience has shown how deeply the element of emotion pervades all our thinking; how persistently it clogs our pursuit and judgment of facts, strain as we may to escape from its net; how persuasively it beguiles our attention away from what we do not wish to see.

By this, too, we can realize more clearly the profound disservice done to Islam by the modernists. So far from guiding Muslim thought into this creative channel, they have fastened on it still more firmly the shackles of the romantic imagination and encouraged it to interpret history in terms of the capricious impulses of the moment.[7] There is no stronger proof of the superficiality of the Western impact upon the Muslim peoples than the fact that the immense revolution in historical thought in the West in the nineteenth century has not yet penetrated into the Muslim world. Nothing is more disconcerting to the student than to find otherwise well-informed followers of Iqbāl mechanically repeating his immature historical judgments or to find modernists in Egypt eagerly seizing on any pronouncements by Western writers, no matter how ill founded, uncritical, or partisan, which chime in with their own sentiments or flatter their pride.

But I do not wish to imply that the way of advance for Muslims lies through the mere taking-over of Western historical method. It is not so at all. The Muslim world must seek, rather, to re-create and build upon the foundations of its own early historical criticism, with the aid of such elements of Western method as it finds applicable and necessary. It has not, as has sometimes been said, to live through the whole evolutionary process of modern Western thought. The slow stages by which the reasoning mind in Europe was purified of its medieval fantasies and reborn under the discipline of natural science may be quite irrelevant to Islamic culture.

The Muslim mind has to traverse a parallel path, traced out for it by the basic character of its own thought.[8] Historical method in the West is still to a large degree under the influence of that scientific determinism which the Muslim mind has always rejected. The Muslim historian, if he builds upon the foundations of Muslim thought, will not be tempted to reduce history to a pattern of abstract concepts; for him concrete facts are always to be viewed in their particular concrete relations, although his vision will include (as the vision of the true historian must include) the workings of a reason higher than that of man.

Can we, finally, observe any indications of a movement of Islamic thought in this direction? They are few enough, indeed, but they exist. On the surface, orthodox circles appear to be devoting most of their energies to formulating a doctrine which in its rigidity and demand for conformity is opposed not only to the revolutionary outlook of the reformers but even to the wise tolerance of Islamic tradition. But it may be that this excess of formalism is itself a sign of uneasiness. It is characteristic of all profound changes of thought that their beginnings are obscure and tentative and oppressed by the great weight of inertia against which they have to struggle. It is of some significance that the greatest of the real reformers in Islam, Shaikh Muhammad Abduh, was deeply influenced by the work and thought of Ibn Khaldūn and that in the teaching of his truest followers the evolutionary concept of historical development is slowly broadening out and overleaping the limitations set upon it by the traditional orthodox doctrine.

But this is only a first step, and the struggle against fundamentalism has still to be fought. It would be presumptuous for us to go further than we have gone. It is the task of Muslims themselves to find the way and to reformulate their principles of belief and action accordingly, a task which will not be completed for many generations and probably not without conflict. Truth must always fight for its existence, and it is not always victorious in the short run.

NOTES AND REFERENCES

PREFATORY NOTE

The following notes are confined to references and some few explanatory or supplementary materials which seemed, for one reason or another, to be out of place in the preceding text. Most of the printed sources in European languages are quoted either in the text or in these notes; but it is to be regretted that files of many journals and a number of other publications since 1939 were not available at the time these lectures were prepared. Among those works to which no direct reference could be made, special acknowledgment is due to the writings of R. G. Collingwood, which have supplied clues to the elucidation of many problems of Islamic religious thought.

CHAPTER I

1. The ulema of al-Azhar now take the view that the use of translations of the Koran for nonliturgical purposes by non-Arab Muslims is permissible (see *Nūr al-Islām* [*Majallat al-Azhar*], II, 122–32; VII, 77–112, 123–34, and a special supplement by Muḥammad Farīd Wagdī entitled *Al-Adilla al-ᶜilmīya ᶜalā jawāz tarjamat maᶜāni'l-Ḳurᵓān*). The opposite view is strongly argued by the Salafi Shaikh Rashīd Riḍā (see above, p. 34) in his treatise, *Tarjamat al-Ḳurᵓān* (Cairo, 1926).

2. Sūra 50:42: *Inna naḥnu nuḥyī wa-numītu wa-ilaina ᵓl-maṣīr.*

3. Cf. *Nūr al-Islām*, II, 487. The main argument advanced in favor of this claim—the existence of a *shūrā*, or consultative council, in the primitive caliphate—no more proves the democracy of Islam than it does that of Hitler. But it does not, of course, follow that political democracy is incompatible with Islam.

4. See the article "Ḳahwa," by C. van Arendonk, in *Encyclopaedia of Islam*.

5. A summary of the main conclusions reached in the long and involved controversy on *ijmāᶜ* will be found in O. Pesle, *Les Fondements du droit musulman* (Casablanca, [1944]), pp. 93–105; see also *Encyclopaedia of Islam, s.v.* "Idjmāᶜ" (D. B. Macdonald). A recent Azhar view is expressed in *Nūr al-Islām*, V, 562–66. The writer denies that *ijmāᶜ* is one of the "roots of the Faith" and asserts that, unless it is supported by proofs furnished from the other "roots," it involves error. Hence it cannot by itself sanction any "innovation," still less contradict the beliefs and practices authorized by Koran or Sunna. This argument is, of course, directed specifically against the modernists.

6. The scope and limitations of *ijtihād* are already the subject of a vast and increasing, but mainly ephemeral, literature. They are frequently discussed in *Nūr al-Islām*, with particular reference to the modernist claims (see esp. I, 37–42, 141; III, 284–86; IV, 391, an interesting statement of the necessity of adaptation to modern developments and of the limitation to this principle imposed by religious doctrine; IV, 170–82, and V, 669–79). The Salafi-reformist view will be found in H. Laoust, *Le Califat dans la doctrine de Rashīd Riḍā* (Beirut, 1938).

7. The religious responsibility of the individual is asserted with particular force by Shaikh Muḥammad ᶜAbduh in his treatise *al-Islām waᵓn-Naṣrānīya*

(3d ed., 1341), pp. 59–64. The following sentences are extracted from this passage: "I say that Islam has not given whether to Caliph or to qāḍī or to muftī or to Shaikh al-Islām the smallest authority in the matter of doctrines and the formulation of rules. Whatever authority is held by any one of these is a civil authority defined by Islamic Law, and it is inadmissible that any of them should claim the right of control over the belief or worship of the individual or should require him to defend his way of thought."

CHAPTER II

1. *Moslem World*, III (1913), 15 ff.

2. A similar dislocation between theory and fact can be observed in the development of doctrine relating to political institutions, but for different reasons (see, e.g., the last paragraph of my article, "Some Considerations on the Sunni Theory of the Caliphate," *Archives de l'histoire du droit oriental*, Vol. III [Brussels, 1939]).

3. Recent Azharite pronouncements on this question conform to a growing tendency to react against the extremer determinist positions taken up by both the antischolastics and the orthodox Ashʿarites, e.g., *Nūr al-Islām*, I, 299–306, and II, 640–42.

4. See especially the introductory chapter to his *Iḥyāʾ*, on the nature of ʿIlm (i.e., knowledge of religious truth), where he criticizes the contemporary theologians for their "deviation from the natural way of truth, their deception by the glittering mirage, and their contentment with the husks of religious knowledge."

5. See *Voyages d'Ibn Batoutah*, I, 215 ff.; *ad-Durar al-Kāmina*, I, 153 ff.; and cf. D. B. Macdonald, *Development of Muslim Theology* (New York, 1903), pp. 273–78. But it is worth noting that Ibn Taimīya had an enthusiastic following among the population of Damascus.

6. This argument will be more fully developed in H. A. R. Gibb and Harold Bowen, "Islamic Society and the West," Prefatory Volume: "Islamic Society in the Eighteenth Century," Part II, chaps. viii and ix, to be published by the Oxford University Press.

7. Even outside the ranks of the Ḥanbalis, there were individual cases of fundamentalist reaction before Ibn ʿAbd al-Wahhāb; see, e.g., Jabarti, I, 48–49, and the note on Muḥammad b. Ismāʿīl aṣ-Ṣanʿānī by J. Schacht in *Zeitschrift für Semitistik*, VI (Leipzig, 1928), 203, with which cf. Brockelmann, *Supplement*, II, 556.

8. *The Reconstruction of Religious Thought in Islam* (2d ed; Oxford, 1934), p. 92.

9. A French translation of this work by Mlle A.-M. Goichon was published at Paris in 1942.

10. T. W. Arnold, *The Preaching of Islam* (2d ed.; London, 1912), p. 327.

11. The *maulids* are described in detail by several of the nineteenth-century travelers in Egypt (see esp. H. Couvidou, *Etude sur l'Egypte contemporaine* [Cairo, 1873], pp. 231–42) and in more general terms by E. W. Lane in his *Manners and Customs of the Modern Egyptians*, see Index, *s.v.* "moolid." The extent to which the puritanical campaign of the ulema and the reformers, aided by the government, has restricted and repressed these popular festivals is deplored in a recent work by Major J. W. McPherson, *The Moulids of Egypt* (Cairo, 1941).

12. See *Rissalat al-Tawhid* (French trans.; Paris, 1925), p. 140. The cult of the saints is a frequent subject of discussion and of polemics in the earlier volumes of

Nūr al-Islām. In opposition to the Wahhābī doctrine, the Azhar shaikhs consistently maintain the lawfulness of recourse to the intercession of the saints and the possibility of miracles (*karāmāt*) by saints, alive or dead.

13. The Salafīya movement has been analyzed in an interesting study by Henri Laoust, "Le Reformisme orthodoxe des Salafiya," *Revue des études islamiques*, Vol. VI (1932). On their polemic with the ulema see, for example, a vigorous attack on Shaikh Rashīd Riḍā in *Nūr al-Islām*, III, 330–40. But on Shaikh Rashīd Riḍā's death a generous tribute was paid to him in VI, 510, acknowledging his learning and his services to Islam, above all in "overthrowing the reign of *taqlīd*, which had imposed upon Muslims a division into two parties, one that remains petrified in its following of traditional usages which are opposed to the spirit of the Faith, and a second group which revolted against Islam and has adopted a way that is not the way of the true Believers."

14. Professor Schacht, in a review of modern Wahhābī literature (*Zeitschrift für Semitistik*, VI, 200–212), has brought out clearly the tendency of modern Wahhābī and philo-Wahhābī writers to emphasize their orthodoxy and their adhesion to the accepted Ḥanbali school.

15. On the *Manār* movement in Algeria see H. A. R. Gibb (ed.), *Whither Islam?* (London, 1932), p. 88, and the journal *L'Afrique française* from 1930 onward; for Indonesia see *Whither Islam?* pp. 268 ff.

16. A brief account of the Ahl-i Ḥadīth is given by Murray Titus, *Indian Islam* (Oxford University Press, 1930), pp. 187–89.

17. M. Ḥusain Haikal, *Zainab* (1st ed.; London, 1914), pp. 320, 322–23.

CHAPTER III

1. Charles C. Adams, *Islam and Modernism in Egypt* (Oxford University Press, 1933), pp. 38–39; *Taʾrīkh al-Ustādh al-Imām*, II, 37–45.

2. Adams, *op. cit.*, pp. 70–78; A. Sékaly, "L'Université d'El-Azhar et ses transformations," *Revue des études islamiques*, I (Paris, 1927), 100–101.

3. See, e.g., an address by the late Rector of al-Azhar, Muḥammad Muṣṭafā al-Marāghi, in *Nūr al-Islām*, VI, 105–7.

4. Al-Azhar was founded on the conquest of Egypt by the schismatic Fatimids in A.D. 969, as a training college for Shiʿite propagandists. Its conversion to an orthodox college dates from the reign of Saladin (1171–93), but it remained in a neglected condition until reconstructed and re-endowed by the Mamluk Sultan Baibars in 1267 (A.H. 665).

5. *Bulletin of the School of Oriental Studies*, IV, Part IV (London, 1928), 757–58. Cited hereafter as "*BSOS*."

6. *Rissalat al-Tawhid*, trans. B. Michel and Moustapha Abdel Razik (Paris, 1925), pp. 107–9; cf. also *ibid.*, pp. 6–7, and Adams, *op. cit.*, pp. 127–33.

7. Adams, *op. cit.*, pp. 134–35.

8. (Oxford University Press, 1929), pp. 36 ff.

9. A first approach to the study of this problem in modern Turkey has been made by H. E. Allen in *The Turkish Transformation* (University of Chicago Press, 1935).

10. It is strange that Professor Macdonald should not have realized that it was because of this that dogmatic theology insisted, with characteristic extremism, upon the tradition: "These are in the Garden, and I care not; and these are in the Fire, and I care not" (see *The Religious Attitude and Life in Islam* [University of Chicago Press, 1906], p. 301). The utilitarian motive must be eliminated from the religious ethic at whatever cost; men are required to do good because they are commanded to do so by God, not in order to gain Paradise.

11. See Henri Laoust in *Revue des études islamiques*, VI (1932), 193–94.

12. Adams, *op. cit.*, pp. 259–67.

13. A. Jeffery in *Der Islam*, XX, 301–8. The report of the Azhar commission which condemned the work was published in *Nūr al-Islām*, II, 163–205 and 249–81.

14. Adams, *op. cit.*, pp. 253–59. For further references see *BSOS*, V, 456–58, and VII, 7, n. 1.

15. A full account of the activities of one of these clubs, the "Y.M.M.A." (*jamᶜiyat ash-shubbān al-muslimīn*), was given by G. Kampffmeyer in H. A. R. Gibb (ed.), *Whither Islam?* (1932), pp. 102–37. The more popular movements which express social discontent in the form of religious societies are dealt with in chap. vi below.

16. See G. Widmer, *Übertragungen aus der neuarabischen Literatur*, Vol. II: *Der iraqische Dichter Ǧamīl Ṣidqī az-Zahāwi* (Berlin, 1935), p. 58.

17. See, e.g., K. G. Saiyidain, *Iqbal's Educational Philosophy* (Lahore, 1938).

18. *The Secrets of the Self*, trans. R. A. Nicholson (London, 1920), ll. 845–48.

19. There is, of course, an extensive Aḥmadi propagandist literature, from translations of the Koran down to fugitive pamphlets. See further an article by Dr. James T. Addison, "The Ahmadiya Movement and Its Western Propaganda," *Harvard Theological Review*, Vol. XXII (1929). The Azhar attitude to the Aḥmadīya movement is illustrated by *Nūr al-Islām*, III, 447–63, and IV, 5–17, 110–19.

CHAPTER IV

1. A peculiar instance is offered by an editorial article in *Nūr al-Islām*, III, 7–20, strongly criticizing the views of the polygraph Muḥammad Farīd Wagdī, who himself became editor of the journal little more than a year later.

2. Wilfred Cantwell Smith, *Modern Islam in India* (Lahore, 1943), pp. 44–45.

3. See I. Goldziher, *Die Richtungen der islamischen Koranauslegung* (Leyden, 1920), pp. 349 ff. It is to the credit of the shaikhs of al-Azhar that, while they argue that "the Koran does not contradict the facts established by science" (*Nūr al-Islām*, II, Part III, 17–23), they reject the attempts made to find "anticipations" of scientific discoveries in the Koran (e.g., V, 411–13).

4. From a "ḥadīth ramaḍān" in *al-Balāgh* (Cairo, October 11–12, 1941). The last sentence of this quotation illustrates the persistence of a characteristic tendency in Muslim thought to view historical persons and events in terms of absolute and predetermined categories.

5. See Tor Andrae, *Die Person Muhammads in Lehre und Glaube seiner Gemeinde* (Stockholm, 1918), esp. chap. vi, "Die Entstehung des Prophetencultus."

6. Smith, *op. cit.*, p. 74.

7. *Moslem World*, IX, (1919), 27. At the same time it must be said that the article by W. H. T. Gairdner, from which this phrase is taken, is a completely justified criticism of the modernist treatment of historical sources.

8. *Op. cit.*, p. 56.

9. This doctrine (based on Sūra 23:102) is held also by the orthodox (cf. *Nūr al-Islām*, II, 215–18, and the [unsatisfactory] article *s.v.* "Barzakh" in the *Encyclopaedia of Islam*).

10. Professor T. W. Manson in *The Interpretation of the Bible* (London, 1944), pp. 92–93.

11. *Ibid.*, p. 102.

12. *Ibid.*, pp. 120–21.

CHAPTER V

1. This was so, even if the conflict was to a great degree softened by the readiness of most Near Eastern peoples to accept Islamic law in preference to the ecclesiastical law of Byzantium or Zoroastrian Persia.

2. I have omitted all discussion of proposals for reform of the Sharᶜī courts and codification of Sharᶜī law, since these concern only modifications of procedure, without affecting the general principles of the administration and application of the religious law (but see also n. 16 below).

3. See A. Sékaly, "Le Probleme des wakfs en Egypte," *Revue des études islamiques*, Vol. III (1929); and J. Schacht in *Der Islam*, XX, 215-23. The reformers distinguish, as a rule, between genuinely charitable *waqfs* (*awqāf khairīya*), intended for the endowment of religious and charitable institutions, and the private or family *waqfs* (*awqāf ahlīya*), intended to benefit a particular family or individual.

4. *Ziya Gökalp: sa vie et sa sociologie*, by Findikoglu Ziyaeddin Fahri (Paris, 1936), p. 240; Iqbāl, *Six Lectures on the Reconstruction of Religious Thought in Islam* (Oxford University Press, 1934), p. 153.

5. The jurists go so far as to admit that local custom may be (or even ought to be) observed when it is not repugnant to a text or indication in the Koran or the prophetic tradition, but not otherwise except under plea of "overriding necessity." An argument similar to that of Ziyā Gök Alp, on a wider scale, was put forward by Jalāl Nūrī Bey in *Ittiḥād-i Islām* (Constantinople, 1913; Arabic trans., Cairo, 1920), pp. 42 ff. The legal view of ᶜurf or ᶜāda is summarized in the official commentary on the *Mejelle*, arts. 36 ff.; and the Azhar view in *Nūr al-Islām*, I, 534-40.

6. *Al-Lubāb* (Baghdad, 1928), p. 126; G. Widmer, *Übertragungen aus der neurarabischen Literatur*, Vol. II: *Der iraqische Dichter Ǧamīl Ṣidqī az-Zahāwi* (Berlin, 1935), p. 38.

7. *Al-Lubāb*, pp. 235-36; Widmer, *op. cit.*, pp. 44-45.

8. See *Oriente moderno*, XI (1931), 39-41; Rudi Paret, *Zur Frauenfrage in der arabisch-islamischen Welt* (Stuttgart, 1934), pp. 17-18.

9. *The Spirit of Islam* (2d ed.; London, 1922), chap. v, pp. 222 ff.

10. This statement is buttressed by reference to two of Hallam's works. *The Constitutional History of England*, I, 87 and note, and *Middle Ages*, p. 353, The passages in question appear to be the following. From the former: "It appears to have been common for the clergy, by licence from their bishops, to retain concubines, who were, Collier says, for the most part their wives." From the latter: "In every country, the secular or parochial clergy kept women in their houses, upon more or less acknowledged terms of intercourse, by a connivance of their ecclesiastical superiors, which almost amounted to a positive toleration." It is difficult to believe that so accomplished a master of English as was Sayyid Amir ᶜAli could have been so unfamiliar with English usage as to assume that the use of the plural in these passages implied a plurality of wives or concubines.

11. It may be noted in passing that this ingenious argument is part of the stock in trade of all feminist and most modernist writers. But it is false, although it has the support of Muhammad ᶜAbduh (*Taʾrikh al-Ustādh al-Imām*, II, 113 ff.), and the doctors of al-Azhar have no difficulty in disproving it and rejecting it outright (*Nūr al-Islām*, II, 564-72; V, 528-29).

12. This unjustifiable and, indeed, foolish attack upon the probity and religious loyalty of the great founders of the schools of law, though not, perhaps, unexpected in a Shiᶜite writer, is also, unfortunately, characteristic of much modernist argument.

13. Sūra 2:228: *walahunna mithlu ᵓlladhī ᶜalaihinna biᵓlmaᶜrūfi waliᵓrrijāli ᶜalaihinna darajatun.*

14. Wilfred Cantwell Smith, *Modern Islam in India* (Lahore, 1943), pp. 80–81.

15. *Ibid.*, p. 165.

16. See, e.g., an article by ᶜAbbās Ṭāhā in *Nūr al-Islām*, VI, 263–69, approving the modifications introduced into family law in Egyptian legislation of 1920 and 1929 (on which see Schacht, *op. cit.*, XX, 223–33). But orthodox writers show no reluctance to defend polygamy and the right of repudiation in principle (e.g., *Nūr al-Islām*, II, 564–72 and 706–13; and Farīd Wagdī, *ibid.*, V, 528–38). The generally similar position of Rashīd Riḍā and the Salafīya is summed up by Henri Laoust in *Le Califat dans la doctrine de Rashīd Riḍā* (Beirut, 1938), p. 262, n. 35; and in fuller detail by Paret, *op. cit.* For India see Smith, *op. cit.*, pp. 79 and 321. The chief weakness in much of this polemic is the argument that the social ethic based upon the Islamic recognition of polygamy is better than that of the Christian law of monogamy corrupted by prostitution. The argument might be accepted if this were a true representation of the facts; but it involves shutting one's eyes to the fact that prostitution has always been and still is widespread in Islamic society, quite apart from the legalization of concubinage with slavewomen.

CHAPTER VI

1. Wilfred Cantwell Smith, *Modern Islam in India* (Lahore, 1943), p. 69.

2. See ᶜAbd ar-Raḥmān al-Kawākibī, *Umm al-Qurā*, final section. So also Jalāl Nūrī Bey in his Pan-Islamic treatise, *Ittiḥād-i Islām* (Constantinople, 1913; Arabic trans., Cairo, 1920), calls for the election of a universal caliph charged with the reform of the Sharīᶜa (p. 45), but subsequently argues that in practice the Imamate of the Ottoman Sultans "has to be accepted" (pp. 255–59).

3. II, 616. (That *Nūr al-Islām* is the official organ of al-Azhar is explicitly stated in VI, 102.)

4. See chap. i, n. 12.

5. At the present stage of development the names, size, and importance of the individual movements are constantly fluctuating. Leading examples at the moment of writing are the Muslim Brotherhood (*Ikhwān Muslimin*) in Egypt and the Khāksārs in India.

6. E.g., *Nūr al-Islām*, I, Part II, 3–9, and Part VII, 500 ff.

7. This is one of the main factors which vitiate any attempt to draw a comparison between the Western Renaissance and the modernist movements in the Islamic world. In the Renaissance (as distinct from the Reformation) the challenge to the doctrines and culture of the medieval church came partly, it is true, from the subjectivism of the newly released sense of individuality but also (and more effectively) from a relatively pure devotion to reason and a belief in its supremacy; whereas Islam and its culture are challenged today by a pseudo-rationalism (as clamorous in the West as in the East) which mistakes emotion for thought and propaganda for argument.

8. Cf. Karl Mannheim, *Man and Society in an Age of Reconstruction* (London and New York, 1940), p. 227: "Never has mankind been able to maintain a level of culture which it had once attained without establishing some sort of continuity with the bearers of the older cultural heritage and their techniques of rationalization and sublimation. Just as a revolution, however radical, should not destroy the machinery of production, if there is not to be a relapse into backward standards of living, so the bearers of the accumulated cultural heritage cannot be cast aside if one wants to avoid a cultural catastrophe."

INDEX